Hope in the Hardest of Places

---

*The Story of
Merle and Louisa Graven*

Louisa Graven

 CHRISTIAN PUBLICATIONS, INC.
CAMP HILL, PENNSYLVANIA

ꞏCHRISTIAN PUBLICATIONS, INC.

3825 Hartzdale Drive, Camp Hill, PA 17011
www.christianpublications.com

Faithful, biblical publishing since 1883

Hope in the Hardest of Places
ISBN: 0-87509-984-X
LOC Control Number: 2003110705

04 05 06 07 08   5 4 3 2 1

NOTE: *All names of persons and places used in this book
were those in use at the time that the events took place.*

Contents

Acknowledgments

These pages have been written to attest to the faithfulness of God and to "tell the next generation/ the praiseworthy deeds of the LORD,/ his power, and the wonders he has done" (Psalm 78:4). The task would have been impossible without the assistance of others, so I express my appreciation to the following:

- My husband, who provided encouragement during the months I wrote and typed.

- Our family, who were supportive and helpful in various ways.

- Dr. Louis L. King, who graciously took the time to read this manuscript and write the foreword for it.

- The several persons who, in one way or another, helped to make possible my getting this manuscript on the computer.

- Marilynne Foster and Gretchen Nesbit for their very helpful advice and editorial expertise in preparing the book for publication.

- All who prayed and supported us during our years of missionary ministry.

Foreword

For as long as most of us can remember, Cambodia has been an inscrutable nation, placidly backward and largely impervious to the gospel message.

Until the communists assumed the reins of government in 1975, Buddhism was the national religion, and the king was the nation's titular head. Ninety-five percent of the population were adherents, and one person out of every seventy-five was a Buddhist priest. Until 1970, when the country became a republic, the king strove to keep Buddhism supreme in the land.

The Christian and Missionary Alliance had the distinction of sending the first Protestant missionary to Cambodia. That was in 1923. For many years thereafter, the C&MA maintained the only evangelical witness there.

In 1933, the government sent to all provincial governors a proclamation restricting missionary activity to those exact locations where missionaries had worked prior to December 31, 1932. This royal proclamation effectively closed more than half of the country to the gospel message. The Cambodians had a proverb: "As goes the king, so go the people." The people, thereafter, considered it non-patriotic, even bordering on disloyalty to the king and to their country, to convert to Christianity. Consequently, only a small number of peasants responded to the invitation to accept Christ. Exceedingly few were willing to suffer the harassment and discrimination that accompanied being a Christian.

World War II and the Japanese occupation came in 1940. Some missionaries were interned, while others escaped to safety. Thus, the work of making Christ known, to a large extent, came to a standstill.

After World War II, the French returned to reestablish their colonial government. An organized nationalist movement known as the Issarak Rebellion sought to oust the French. The eight years of Issarak activity kept the country in a state of disruption and terror more difficult than anything experienced during the Japanese occupation. This continued until the French departed in 1954.

It was during the last four years of the Issarak Rebellion that the Graven family began their missionary service in Cambodia.

In 1965, Prince Sihanouk expelled the missionaries, closed all churches, forbade Christians to congregate for worship and, on pain of imprisonment, forbade pastors to preach.

Five years later, the government changed course again and lifted the ban on the propagation and open practice of Christianity. A review of the mission and church statistical reports from the beginning in 1923 to 1970 shows that only 698 persons had been baptized, of whom less than 400 were then alive. Cambodia had proved to be a very difficult and unresponsive mission field.

Then suddenly, from mid-1970 to April 1975, an incredible number of Cambodians turned to Christ. The number of churches in the city of Phnom Penh grew from 2 to 29, with an approximate total of 10,000 believers. Among them were the director of the national museum, the commissioner of the national police, the composer of the music of the Cambodian national anthem, the president of the supreme court, two university professors, many university students and a large number of soldiers and refugees.

As far as I know, no Alliance missionary who lived and served in Cambodia both during the dangerous part of the Issarak Rebellion as well as the brief four-and-one-half years (1970-1975) of the mighty acts of God has chronicled his or her experiences for the public to read. Thankfully, Louisa Graven has now done so.

In her story, Mrs. Graven has managed to weave an epic tapestry that meshes together many details of what life and service in "the hardest of places" meant for her and her family over the many years they lived in Cambodia.

In this deeply moving narrative, Mrs. Graven describes her pilgrimage from childhood up until retirement. Her conversion, call to missionary service, educational and service preparation, courtship and marriage to Merle Graven, the Gravens' singleness of purpose, raising children on the mission field, hardships of life, health crises and finally the amazing years of the great and mighty revival are taken one after the other. Reminiscent of the style and scope of the best of missionary autobiographies, this is a book that will bring spiritual good to the reader.

Louis L. King, D.D., past president,
The Christian and Missionary Alliance

1

God Will Make a Way

As the sun cast its beams across the azure sky and the sparkling blue waters of the South China Sea, the SS *Steel Rover* sliced steadily toward its next port of call, Saigon, Vietnam. Forty-four days earlier, on Friday, January 14, 1949, we had sailed peacefully out of the New York harbor, the ship loaded with freight and scheduled to stop at various seaports around the world. In addition to officers and crew, the ship was equipped to accommodate twelve passengers. But, for the next three weeks we—Merle and Louisa Graven and our three-year-old daughter, Marilyn—would be the only passengers on board.

We had anticipated sailing three months earlier, but since I had no birth certificate, my passport had been delayed. Having already resigned his pastorate, my husband, Merle, had accepted speaking engagements in various churches until our rescheduled departure. We did not know it then, but God had a specific plan for us to be on that particular ship.

The ship's passengers ate in the officers' dining room, where we enjoyed a pleasant atmosphere and well-planned, appealing menus each day. That was where we met "Gary," who would be our waiter for the next several weeks. Gary was a tall, dark-haired, gregarious young man, who often lingered to chat a bit at the table as he served us. We also had frequent opportunities for brief conversations with him on deck.

One day, Gary revealed to us that his grandfather was a widely known pastor and his father was president of a university. But Gary had chosen, temporarily at least, to be a nightclub singer. Doubtless many prayers had ascended to God on his behalf! And those prayers were answered in a quite spectacular way some time later.

It began, Gary told us, one evening when he was away from home. While he was gone, an artist friend drew a phosphorescent picture of Jesus Christ on Gary's bedroom wall.

"I came home that night," Gary said, "very much under the influence of alcohol. I went to bed and switched off the light. Suddenly, there was Jesus Christ looking down at me. Stunned and frightened, I leaped out of bed and turned on the light. Christ was gone. Returning to bed and switching off the light, I saw Him again. I quickly exited the room and slept elsewhere that night.

"The following morning," Gary continued, "I discovered the secret and surmised who had done it." Angry and annoyed by this friendly prank gone bad, Gary decided to get a job on a ship, take a trip around the world and get away from it all.

That was how we met Gary, and Merle and I wondered if God had arranged for our paths to cross. How surprised Gary must have been to find that the only passengers he had to serve three times a day were missionaries!

After two weeks, perhaps he had had enough, because when the ship docked at Los Angeles, Gary got off, went to a nightclub and signed on for a job as a singer. To fulfill his contract on the ship, however, he would have to remain on the ship until we reached San Francisco, then fly back to Los Angeles. While serving our dinner one evening, Gary told Merle his plans.

"Does it have a future?" Merle asked.

"No," Gary answered.

Reaching into his shirt pocket, Merle handed Gary a tract that we had been given while walking down a street in Los Angeles. The tract was titled " 'Good-Night' or 'Good-Bye,' Which?" It was the story of a dying Christian who called his family together to bid them farewell. To his wife and grown children—except his youngest son—he simply said, "Good-night." But to his youngest, he said, "Good-bye."

"Why, Dad, did you say good-night to the others but good-bye to me?" the young man wanted to know.

"Because they have put their trust in God," the father replied. "I'll see them again in the morning. But you have been a disappointment to me, son. I have no hope of ever seeing you again. So it's good-bye to you." Then the grief-stricken son accepted Christ as his Savior.

"You might find this hard to believe," Merle said, "but this tract was given to me on the street in L.A. I would like to share it with you."

Gary took the tract and stuck it in his pocket. We later learned that when he returned to his room, he stuffed it into a magazine. Some time later, he picked up the magazine again, the tract fell out and he read it. God was quietly at work even though Gary would not likely have wanted to admit it.

When the ship set sail from San Francisco, Gary was still on board. He had called the nightclub in Los Angeles and canceled his contract.

The first week on board the *Steel Rover,* Merle had been asked if he would be interested in conducting Sunday services. So, each Sunday thereafter, when the ship was at sea, there was a service held for all aboard.

Privately we were praying that Gary would yield to the wooing of the Holy Spirit. Though he attended the Sunday services, he had not yet shown any visible sign of response. Now, more than six weeks had passed, and we would soon be leaving the ship.

On Sunday, February 27, 1949, we watched as the outline of Cap Saint-Jacques (a port now called Vung Tau [pronounced Voom Tao]) came into view. Vung Tau is located near the end of an eleven-mile-long piece of land that juts into the South China Sea and partially encloses Ganh Rai Bay, which is fed by the Saigon River. A lighthouse stood sole guard at this entrance to South Vietnam, and an awesome feeling welled up within our hearts as we recalled the beautiful way in which God had woven the threads of our lives together and brought us to this point.

I was born in the hills of West Virginia, where my father's great-grandparents settled in 1840 after having emigrated from the Black Forest region of

Germany. For perhaps a hundred years, a sizeable area in what is now the Exchange and the Chapel communities of Braxton County, West Virginia, was widely known as the German Settlement. A log church was erected there and used until a new German Church, later known as the Otterbein Chapel, was dedicated in 1885. It still exists today.

My father, Lonnie Gerwig, was a World War I veteran who served overseas. His task had been hauling ammunition to the front lines using a wagon and horses. My mother, Alice Queen Moyers, was also born and reared in Braxton County. Her maternal grandmother was Elizabeth Boone Belknap, known as Betsy. Family tradition says that Betsy's father, Jacob Boone, Sr., was a grandson of the legendary pioneer Daniel Boone. At the age of fourteen, Alice was converted during a revival service in the little schoolhouse which at that time served as both church and school.

After young Lonnie Gerwig returned from Europe, he and Alice were married and lived on Tom's Run across the creek from the lovely home my grandfather had built. A stony creek bed was the only road.

When I was two years old, my father moved his family to Ohio, because he thought there would be more accessible schools there. Soon thereafter, a baby boy joined the family. In all that time, God had already begun a chain of events to accomplish His purpose for my life. We attended Sunday school and church regularly. One of my earliest memories is learning to pray at my mother's knee.

My childhood years were happy and carefree. I loved the warm summer days when I could roam barefoot around the farm and smell the marvelous aroma of new-mown hay. Nostalgic memories of playing in the barn, walking on stilts, climbing the big shade tree in the front lawn and having picnics on the wagon with my brother, Aaron, still replay in my mind.

The country school was approximately three-fourths of a mile from our home. The unpaved road led past a wooded area and became very muddy at times in the winter. Aaron and I would plod through the wet snow with cold, raw wind stinging our faces and hands. Then the country school closed and we were bussed to a nearby town. My father sold the farm and we moved.

A Christian and Missionary Alliance church was later planted in Ashland, Ohio, a few miles from our home. The small congregation was still meeting up-stairs over a poolroom when we were invited to at-tend some evangelistic meetings. I was sixteen, a high-school senior.

After returning home from service one night, I said to Mother, "Please pray for me." I felt the need for a definite assurance of salvation. There in my bedroom, I yielded to God and found that assurance. Approxi-mately three months later, my cousin, Frances Bender (Mrs. Tom Owens), invited me to spend a weekend at Beulah Beach Bible Conference. I sat, fascinated, as I listened to stories of missionary adventure. When an invitation for dedication was extended to the youth on Saturday evening, I arose from the back of the taber-nacle and made my way to the altar. I had no idea then that my decision would drastically change the course of my life.

Shortly after returning home, I experienced something very unusual: I had the same dream for three nights in a row. In my dream, everything outside was covered with a blanket of snow—but it was the month of August. I couldn't understand how that could be. When I awoke after the third dream, I sat up in bed and looked out the window. For a fleeting moment, everything appeared white. Realizing it was another dream, I lay back down and said, "What is the meaning of this?" Immediately this message came to my heart: "The harvest is white. The laborers are few. Go ye into the harvest" (see Matthew 9:38).

My goal had always been to be a teacher. However, during my senior year of high school, I had elected to take all business subjects. I excelled in bookkeeping and had even won a district bookkeeping contest. I decided to become an accountant—that is, until the high school principal approached me and asked, "What do you plan to do after graduation?"

"I plan to attend a business college," I replied.

"I cannot obtain a scholarship for you at a business college," he told me. "However, if you choose to attend a liberal arts college, I will help you obtain a scholarship."

I decided to take advantage of the opportunity and enrolled at Ashland College (now called Ashland University). I planned to study elementary education. But as time passed, I realized that God was still speaking to me, prompting me to do something else. My heart was responsive. "Whenever you open the door, Lord," I promised, "I will go to the Missionary Training Institute" (Nyack College).

God gave me this promise in Habakkuk 2:3: "For the revelation awaits an appointed time. . . . Though it linger, wait for it; it will certainly come and will not delay." So after graduation from Ashland, I taught school for a year in Lexington, Ohio. At the close of the school year, the superintendent brought me a contract to renew my position for the following year. I took it back to my rented room to seek an answer from the Lord.

While reading First Samuel 20, I felt that God was speaking directly to me—it was time to go to Nyack. I recall walking down the long hall at school the following morning with trepidation. How would the superintendent react? What would he say? I returned the unsigned contract and told him about my plan.

"You are very foolish," he responded.

At the end of the school year, I went home. Within days, there was a knock at my door. It was a member of the school board from my hometown of Nankin. "We have a vacancy in the school this year," he said. "Would you be interested in the position?" I did not accept.

When my father heard that I had turned down two teaching opportunities, especially the one near home, he was extremely disappointed. Since I was determined to go to Nyack, he said angrily, "Then go, but you can expect no financial support from me."

I had saved enough, I thought, for one year at Nyack. After that, I would have to wholly trust the Lord. But what about clothes? A pretty new dress? Such thoughts were only daydreams. I simply couldn't afford them.

"What about that pretty formal that you wore in college?" Mother asked one day. "Let's ask your Aunt

Ethel if she can transform it into a street dress for you." That became my "special" dress at Nyack.

I loved the school. It seemed to me that it was the nearest thing to heaven on earth. But, when I went to register for the second semester, I discovered that I did not have quite enough money to finish out the year. I was not to be deterred, though. Even though I knew about the strict rules, I went to the dean of women and asked to move out of the dorm and work in a home for my room and board. She denied permission.

I returned to my room very disappointed and discouraged. On my knees, I cried out to God, "Did you bring me here, Lord, only to forsake me now? Did I forgo those two teaching opportunities only to have to leave the school?" I prayed until I gained victory over my despair. Then I arose, walked directly to my desk and wrote the following lines:

> Shall I doubt the Master's leading
> When He's been so good to me?
> Shall I worry any longer
> About the obstacles I see?
> Shall I hesitate to trust Him
> With my life, my cares, my all?
> No, I'll question Him no longer,
> Without Him, I'm sure to fall.
>
> Shall I always ask a reason
> Why the way He chose 'tis so?
> Shall I say, "I'll step no farther
> Till the path I clearly know"?
> Shall I fear the unknown future,
> All the steps I cannot see?
> No, I'll venture out with Jesus
> For I know He'll walk with me.

Shall I fail to trust His promise,
"I'll go with thee to the end"?
Shall I with uncertain footsteps
Down the road without Him wend?
Shall I compromise with Satan,
Choosing pleasures first each day?
No, my choice is ever Jesus,
I'll go with Him all the way.

Shall I answer at His bidding,
And into the harvest go?
Is it worth the toil and labor
Leading souls from sin and woe?
Yes, it pays to serve my Jesus
Every step along the way.
When my toiling here is ended,
All I've spent He will repay.

A few days later, I had an idea. I would ask to withdraw the money I had paid in for teacher retirement in Ohio. The request was granted, and when the check arrived, it was the exact amount I needed to pay the balance due on my school bill.

At the end of the school year I went home penniless. Jobs were very scarce and workers were being laid off. Finally, I was able to get employment at a factory where I had worked during a previous summer. But I too was laid off eventually. How could I possibly return to Nyack? Yet there was peace in my heart. Somehow, God would make a way. And then He did something more wonderful than I could have anticipated: He spoke to my father's heart.

"Louisa, if you want to return to Nyack and can find work there, I will supply each month what you lack," my father said. My request for work at the school was granted. God had honored my step of faith.

* * * *

Merle was born in Ashland County, Ohio, the only child of Wellington and Clara Schaffer Graven. As a lad on the farm, his main tasks after school each day were to feed the chickens, gather the eggs, then clean and grade about sixty dozen eggs to send to market.

He had a pet pig, Susie, that had been given to him by a neighbor. He had brought her home in a basket and hand-fed her. Sometimes Susie was permitted to roam unrestrained on the farm. If she wandered too far, Merle would call, "Susie, come back here," and Susie would lift up her head as though to answer, "I hear you," then come running back. Merle decided to take Susie to the county fair. In grooming her, he scrubbed so hard with a strong soap that she blistered. Nevertheless, Susie won the second-prize ribbon.

There was also the old swimming hole in the creek where Merle and his friends would swim on hot summer days, the occasional horseback rides and sledding in winter snows (Merle's sled was always the fastest). Throughout his active childhood, he managed to escape possible death on three different occasions.

The first narrow escape was on a summer day when Merle was about five years old. The hay had been mowed and windrowed and was being gathered into the barn. As the long, sharp prongs extending from the cylinder of the old-fashioned hay loader picked up the hay and moved it to the top, Merle's father waited with a pitchfork to load the hay onto the wagon. Merle was following the hay loader on foot. Suddenly, he was picked up by the prongs along with the hay. Fortunately, his father saw him and called for his mother to stop the horses. Merle had miraculously escaped being pierced by the sharp prongs of the hay loader.

Then, when Merle was thirteen years old, he developed severe abdominal pains one morning at school. The teacher gave him permission to go home. The one-mile walk across fields seemed so long, and several times along the way he had to stop to lie down. Finally he arrived home and his parents drove him to a doctor.

It was the day after Easter, so the doctor dismissed the illness as nothing serious, saying, "The boy ate too many Easter eggs."

By Wednesday morning Merle was critically ill. Another doctor made a house call. Touching Merle's side, he said to his mother, "Which ambulance do you want? We must get him to the hospital immediately."

Merle's mother, though a regular church attender, did not yet know the Lord. Fearing Merle might not survive, she called her pastor and asked him to come quickly and baptize Merle before the ambulance arrived.

It turned out that Merle's appendix was filled with gangrene and was ready to burst. The doctor later testified that he normally began cutting the diseased organ at a certain place, but that time, for some unknown reason, he felt directed to start at the opposite end. "That decision saved Merle's life," he later told the family.

Merle's third near-death experience happened when a group of young people were on their way to camp. Merle was riding in a convertible with two other teens, one of whom was driving. At a speed of sixty miles an hour, the driver was in the process of passing another car. Suddenly, a third car appeared over a knoll. A head-on collision was certain! The teenaged driver turned onto the berm, went down an embankment, bounced around and came back up onto the road. Merle was sitting by a door; it flew open. There were no seat belts but, miraculously, the car did not flip nor were any of the teens thrown from the car. They had all been spared.

God's purpose for sparing Merle soon became evident. One day he was turning the dial on a new radio his parents had bought. He heard the voice of a widely known radio preacher, so he stopped momentarily to listen. Though Merle did not comprehend all he was hearing, tears began to flow down his face and he turned his head so no one could see. The Holy Spirit was beginning to move in his heart.

Some months later, at the age of seventeen, Merle accepted the Lord at an evangelistic service. His conversion was genuine and his lifestyle was immediately transformed. He loved sports, especially basketball and baseball, and he was playing on a baseball team that always had its games on Sunday. However, when he became a Christian, he chose not to play on the Lord's day and immediately quit the team. In the meantime, his mother had accepted Christ as her Savior, and his father did so later.

Merle's goal was to study business in college and eventually own an automobile agency. But first he planned to work for a year. He became an apprentice in a printing company. During that year, the youth of the Ashland Christian and Missionary Alliance Church invited him to go Christmas caroling, and he began to attend the church.

One night he dreamed that he was attending his own high school graduation. The auditorium was filled with people and he was one of the speakers. When he rose to speak, he began to preach. At the conclusion, he gave an invitation and many people came to the front, but Merle didn't know how to lead them to the Lord. He awoke with a start. Though he put little credence in dreams, that particular one haunted him for days. Finally, he said, "Yes, Lord, I'll give my life to serve you." The following fall he enrolled in the Missionary Training Institute (Nyack College).

Merle and I began dating approximately a month before he left to study at Nyack. Eventually, we became engaged. The missionary flame that was lit in my heart at Beulah Beach Bible Conference began to burn more brightly.

I wanted to be a missionary, but Merle wanted to be a stateside pastor and evangelist. We earnestly sought the Lord concerning His will. We also sought the advice of one of our godly professors, who quoted these words to us from Psalm 32:8-9: "I will instruct you and teach you in the way you should go;/ I will counsel you and watch over you./ Do not be like the horse or the mule,/ which have no understanding." We both felt assured that God had brought us together.

Merle became youth pastor of the Havelock Church (now Rosemont Church) in Lincoln, Nebraska. After we married, he was extended a call to become pastor of the Gospel Tabernacle in Fremont, Nebraska (later renamed The Christian and Missionary Alliance Church).

We both enjoyed the pastorate. I was involved in several ministries of the church, and in addition to his pastoral duties, Merle began a weekly radio broadcast and took further study at a local seminary. He and Vernon Neigenfind, a pastor friend from Omaha, started Sunday afternoon services in Blair, Nebraska. During that time we were blessed with our firstborn, a lovely baby daughter whom we named Marilyn Jean.

Merle also had a burden for church planting. While contemplating this possibility, a small independent church in Oak Park, Illinois, which was preparing to become a part of The Christian and Missionary Alliance, extended a call for Merle to become its pastor, and he accepted the challenge. As his work in this new church progressed, plans were being formulated to build a new church building. Meanwhile, I was continuing to pray privately concerning overseas service.

One noon hour, Merle came home from the church office and said, "While I was reading the Word this morning, God spoke to my heart through Second Corinthians 10:16. I heard the Lord saying, 'You have preached missions, you have promoted missions, but you have never given yourself for missions.' I believe that we should at least make ourselves available for foreign service. How do you feel?" It was just what I had been waiting for!

Yet even as we applied for foreign service, there was something that cast a shadow over my joy. Several weeks previously, my mother had suffered a severe stroke. She lay for a while in a coma, and the doctor gave the family no hope for her survival. She was only fifty-one years old. My parents had moved to Marion,

Ohio, and had later made their home available for the initial services to plant a Christian and Missionary Alliance church there. Mother was preparing to host a ladies' meeting the week that she was stricken.

Though she eventually regained consciousness, she was paralyzed on the right side, and her speech was affected. She would never walk again. Mother was dismissed from the hospital as an invalid, and my father hired someone to care for her at home. How could I tell my dear mother that her only daughter was planning to go so far away?

But Mother was a woman of great faith. "If I am going to live, I will walk," she said.

One Sunday afternoon my father lifted Mother from the bed and carried her to a chair. Suddenly Mother announced, "I am going to walk today." She instructed my father and my brother, Aaron, to lift her from the chair while her sister, who was visiting, read from God's Word. Though fearful that Mother might fall and injure herself, they granted her request.

After she was dragged across the room and turned around, she began to take steps. She continued to walk for over thirty-five more years until the Lord took her home at the age of eighty-six. "Ah, Sovereign LORD, you have made the heavens and the earth by your great power and outstretched arm. Nothing is too hard for you" (Jeremiah 32:17).

When I told Mother that Merle and I were planning to go overseas, she replied, "I'm not surprised. I've been expecting it."

My dream to be a missionary was about to be fulfilled.

2

A Promise Fulfilled

As the *Steel Rover* slowly sailed up the winding Saigon River, we stood on deck and marveled at the beauty of this strange land that was halfway around the world from our home. Trees, whiskered and bearded with air plants, branched high along the riverside. Beneath them was a tangle of creepers, thorns and underbrush. Occasionally we caught a glimpse of a thatched-roof house in a nearby clearing. A Vietnamese native clad in black, pajama-like clothing and wearing a cone-shaped straw hat paddled by in a little canoe. We were nearing the end of our journey.

There had been both unpredictable and rewarding experiences over the course of our six-week trip, both on the seas and during the on-shore excursions we took at every port. Our first stop had been Newport News, Virginia, and from there we had sailed the beautiful blue Caribbean Sea with its white-foamed waves. Then, as the ship slowly made its way through the locks of the Panama Canal, a vendor selling bananas had paddled by in a small boat, and Merle bought a large cluster of over 100 bananas for 50 cents and shared them with the crew.

In the Los Angeles area, we had stayed overnight with a pastor friend and his family. Merle spoke the following morning in the worship service, and Marilyn had such an enjoyable time playing with the pastor's three children that she didn't want to go back on the boat. Several other passengers boarded the ship in San Francisco, including Vonnie Morscheck, who was bound for Indonesia, and Paul and Phyllis Davis and their two small children, who were en route to Thailand.

One of the highlights of our trip was the picturesque drive we took around the beautiful Hawaiian island of Oahu. At Pearl Harbor we were reminded of World War II.

Another day, while in the midst of the Pacific Ocean, we felt the ship suddenly change course. "What's the problem?" Merle asked the crew. We were told that a mine had been spied in the water up ahead. Then, in Manila harbor we saw the tops of sunken ships protruding out of the water. Scenes of the destruction caused during World War II were still evident in Manila, though most of the debris had been removed. A cemetery with row after row of white crosses silently chronicled the story of young American soldiers who had paid the supreme sacrifice to ensure our freedom. We had already seen and experienced so much, and we hadn't even reached our final destination!

As our ship pulled up to the dock in Saigon, we scanned the faces of those standing below. No Caucasian faces were among them; no one was waiting to meet us. What could we do? We were in a foreign land where we knew no one and where there would be few, if any, people who knew our language. We had no idea where the mission guesthouse was. How could we possibly find it?

It was 6:30 p.m., local time. A voice soon came over the ship's intercom, announcing, "Because of war conditions in the country, there is a curfew that will take effect in one half hour. If there is no one here to meet you, you must remain on board the ship tonight."

Well, at least we had a place to sleep, but what a disappointment! Weeks before, I had pictured the excitement of having friends and loved ones stand at the dock and wave their good-byes as the ship pulled out of the New York harbor. Then I had imagined missionary colleagues waiting for us at the end of our journey, waving a cheerful welcome to us as we sailed into the harbor. We had experienced neither. It was not until our third day on board the ship in New York that loading was finally completed and we pulled away from the dock. There had been no one to wave that last good-bye. Instead, the three of us had stood alone on deck, staring at the Statue of Liberty until it disappeared from view. And now we had arrived and found no one waiting to receive us.

We knew that our new home was a land embroiled in internal warfare, but we did not know what the future held. We knew only that we were going at the bidding of our Master, following His perfect plan and purpose for our lives. As we stood there in the fading light, we couldn't have predicted God's special plan for that night.

As we were making our way to our cabin to wait until morning, one of the ship's officers approached Merle. "None of the crew can get off the ship and go into town because of the curfew," he said. "We have nothing to do on board tonight. Would you want to hold another service?" Merle was delighted. And, best of all, God was giving Gary one more opportunity to respond to His still, small voice.

That night after the message and invitation, Gary, along with a few others, indicated a desire to make a decision for Christ. God, not circumstances, had planned our overnight stay on board that ship!

The next morning we repacked our suitcases and waited. Surely someone would come that day to meet us. But no one arrived. "I must make an attempt to find the guesthouse," Merle told me.

Several pedicab drivers were at the dock waiting hopefully for a fare. (The pedicab, called a *cyclo* [SEE-klo], is a small, three-wheeled, hooded passenger vehicle in which the passenger sits in front in an open armchair while the driver pedals from behind.) Merle found a driver who understood the words *Mission Evangelique.* Could Merle trust him to know where the mission house was actually located? What if he found himself lost in a city of more than 2 million people? But something had to be done, so off they went, weaving in and out of the constant stream of traffic.

When Merle arrived at the door of the mission guesthome and introduced himself, Rev. E.F. Irwin was surprised and startled. "When did you arrive?" he exclaimed. "We weren't expecting you for several more days." Since the ship had omitted two stops from its original schedule, we had arrived early. Merle returned for us and we finally arrived at the guesthouse that was to be our home for the next few days.

Our first night in the city was never to be forgotten. As evening shadows fell, clouds of mosquitoes emerged from seemingly nowhere to become our relentless pursuers, and we were grateful for the mosquito netting that covered our beds. Innumerable dogs barked through the night, one answering another's howl, and I awoke once at the sound of a strange noise that I could not identify. I learned the next morning that it was a nocturnal insectivorous lizard called a Tokay gecko. This largest specie of the geckos emits a sound similar to the groan of a sick person. Its distinct voice utters seven staccato calls of *tok-ay,* starting loud and winding down to silence. Though noisy at times, this native to southeast Asia is harmless and useful in devouring mosquitoes and other insects.

Saigon was a lovely city of the Orient. Built in the nineteenth and twentieth centuries when Vietnam was under French administration, it was the commercial center for the southern part of Vietnam. Wide, tree-lined boulevards and public parks with endless varieties of tropical foliage and beautiful flowers added to the grandeur of the city. Over the arched gateways that led to most of the French homes in the city were flowering bougainvillea vines with masses of brilliant purple or red floral bracts. The Vietnamese women, slight and graceful, were particularly attractive, clad in their white trousers and long-sleeved, high-collared silk tunics, their black hair pulled back and worn in a knot.

One evening after dinner, as several of us sat around the table conversing, three shots were suddenly heard in the distance, an unwelcome reminder that we were in a country at war. It was the custom of our missionary host to read portions of Scripture from *Daily Light on the Daily Path* each morning and evening. We exchanged glances as he began to read:

> We were troubled on every side; without were fightings, within were fears. Fear not: for they that be with us are more than they that be with them. [Be] strong in the Lord, and in the power of His might.
>
> Thou comest to me with a sword, and with a spear, and with a shield: but I come to thee in the name of the LORD of hosts, the God of the armies of Israel, whom thou hast defied. God is my strength and power: . . . he teacheth my hands to war; so that a bow of steel is broken by mine arms. Our sufficiency is of God.
>
> The angel of the LORD encampeth round about them that fear him, and delivereth them. Behold, the mountain was full of horses and chariots of fire round about Elisha.
>
> The time would fail me to tell of . . . those who through faith subdued kingdoms, . . . out of weakness were made strong, waxed valiant in fight, turned to flight the armies of the aliens.[1]

These words, which I was to recall many times in the days ahead, were God's promise and encouragement to my own heart.

Note

1. Jonathan Bagster, *Daily Light on the Daily Path: A Devotional Textbook for Every Day of the Year, in the Very Words of Scripture,* March 5 [on-line], n.d. July 9, 2003. Available from: <http://www.mun.ca/rels/restmov/texts/dasc/DLDP0 000.HTM>.

3

Perfect Timing

Soaring over the lowlands of Vietnam in a DC-3, we looked down upon the winding river below, its countless little waterfalls dropping gently over the rocks. We were on our way to the mountain town of Dalat where we had been assigned to begin our French language study. Rev. D.I. Jeffrey, the field chairman for French Indochina, accompanied us.

Vietnam's terrain is made up of deltas covered with dense forests and tropical jungles. Mountain ranges run north and south, and fertile plains in the deep valleys are watered by numerous rivers and streams.

At the time, Vietnam, Cambodia and Laos comprised the territory known as French Indochina. All three countries combined were just a little larger than the state of Texas. Vietnam covered less than half of the French Indochina territory but made up about four-fifths of the population.

For decades France had been the protector of all three countries. Thus, French was the official government language, and since we were under appointment to Cambodia, learning French was our first task.

Dalat was a lovely French resort town approximately 5,200 feet above sea level. It was there that the school for missionary children was located and also where the missionaries came for their annual conference and vacation.

Located on a high plateau in the Langbian Mountains, Dalat was an ideal place for the school. When the property was purchased in 1929 it was nothing but jungle. Tall pines had to be felled and a site for each building leveled off. The first building was dedicated on February 10, 1930. This marked the beginning of the mission compound at Dalat. On nearby land, known as the "vacation property," the mission built two chalets and several missionaries built private cottages.

Looking down from the plane, we could see the wreckage of another plane that had crashed on this same route. We saw native villages in clearings scattered throughout the jungle, and at one point a horde of unidentifiable black animals emerged from the trees. Then, suddenly, we moved through a beautiful formation of clouds, and the pilot skillfully guided the plane to a safe landing.

It was March 1949. The climate was delightful. Mornings and evenings were cool, and by midday it was pleasantly warm. I loved the fresh, invigorating, pine-scented air. The sun bathed the mountains with its radiance by day; then, as the moon slowly rose from the midst of the trees, nature seemed at rest and all was well with the world. But we knew that in other areas of Vietnam the Viet Minh guerrillas were active. Each of the three protectorates of

Indochina was now striving for complete independence.

Upon our arrival, I was asked to substitute for a newly appointed teacher for the lower grades who was awaiting her visa. French language study would have to wait. We moved into two rooms in the annex behind the school's kitchen and next to the laundry room.

One day shortly after we arrived, I entered the laundry room to do some washing. A young Vietnamese man, an employee of the school, was doing laundry, and he was humming tunes that I recognized immediately. Then he burst into song in his native tongue, singing "Are You Washed in the Blood?" My heart was deeply moved, for I was witnessing firsthand the fruit of missions. One of the most genuinely exhilarating life experiences is hearing the old hymns of the church sung by a strange people in a foreign tongue. What positive encouragement for a new missionary!

The school enrollment was less than thirty at that time. I was responsible for ten students in grades one through four and for one subject in the fifth grade. Herbert and Lydia Jackson were the houseparents at the school, "Uncle" and "Auntie" to all of the students. The missionary kids (MKs) enjoyed sports, picnics and outings and well-planned fun times.

One of my students, a handsome lad with a happy-go-lucky spirit and a contagious smile, had a habit of never having lessons finished on time, and occasionally I spent extra time after school helping him with math. On April 1 I was working at my desk early in the morning before classes began. Suddenly the door behind me opened and a boy's voice called out, "Mrs. Graven, I have my arithmetic lesson done."

"You have?" I exclaimed quizzically.

"April fool," he said.

"You would have fooled me more if it were done," I replied with a grin.

Teaching at the school was so enjoyable that those twelve weeks seemed like the blink of an eye. Marilyn, too, was very happy with all the attention she got from the students. A Vietnamese *amah* (nurse) cared for her while I taught. One day Marilyn came to class and showed me which seat she wanted when she came to school in another two years.

On Good Friday, most of the older students went down to Djiring, a town fifty miles south of Dalat, to swim and camp overnight in a French house that was in the process of being constructed. Herb Jackson rented a bus to carry the students and their bedding and provisions. Merle and another missionary went along as chaperones.

While the evening meal was being prepared in the light of one lone candle, the freshly boiled water was set in a pail of other water to cool. Later, one of the men came by looking for a drink. "Where is the drinking water?" he asked.

"Over there in the pail," someone replied, unaware that the container of boiled water had been removed. The missionary innocently proceeded to drink water from the scrub pail. Others joined him. "Why does this water taste so soapy?" they complained.

In the darkness, their mistake was discovered too late!

After school closed and the annual missionary conference had ended, I joined Merle in French language study. We moved to a cottage situated on the nearby vacation property. The upstairs living area consisted of a living/dining room, one bedroom and a bathroom. The kitchen was below on the walkout level. From our living area, we could look down over towering pines to a Vietnamese village scattered over a rolling hill.

The months of language study were enjoyable, but at last the time came for us to move on. It was January 1950, and we had been in Dalat for about ten months. A convoy was heading to Saigon on Thursday, January 19, and permission was obtained for us to join it. We had been appointed to Cambodian language study in Battambang, Cambodia's second largest city. The journey would be accomplished in three stages, with the whole trip totaling approximately 520 miles.

With our miniature French Renault loaded to the brim, we left on Wednesday for the town of Djiring. The journey was uneventful, and we spent the night there with missionaries George and Harriette Irwin. Arising before daylight the following morning, we ate breakfast and drove to Blao, further down the mountain, where the convoy was to assemble.

We were well aware of the fact that convoys were subject to ambush by guerrillas along the way, for we had heard stories of such attacks and the atrocities that had been committed. Private cars were usually placed near the head of the convoy in groups of three with armored cars at each end.

When the convoy was finally in order, we were on our way. Rarely did we see another vehicle either ahead of or behind us while we traveled. Now and then we caught a glimpse of a soldier, passed a fort with a tower stockaded by high fence and thickly strung barbed wire or met a military vehicle. Occasionally a tank sat by the side of the road manned by soldiers poised for action.

The convoy moved at a snail's pace. Large holes, presumably caused by enemy bombs and land mines, had not been repaired. The roads were even worse in the more dangerous areas because the populace was afraid to work on them for fear of reprisal.

Marilyn, clutching her doll, had one small corner of the back seat of the car. As we bounced around and over the potholes, items in the car began to shift and fall around her, even hitting her on the head.

Trees and dense brush hemmed us in on either side as we descended the mountain. We passed beautiful wild orchids and tall bamboo trees from which furniture and many other items are made in that part of the world.

"How enjoyable such a trip would be if all were peaceful and normal," remarked Merle.

As we approached the low country where the guerrillas were particularly active, I became increasingly apprehensive. To add to my fear, we suddenly saw in the distance three persons by the side of the road. "Will these be friends or foes?" I wondered aloud. There was nothing we could do but proceed. Fortunately, they were only civilians.

The day grew hotter and there was no opportunity for us to stop and refresh ourselves, so we were greatly relieved when, approximately eight hours later, we arrived safely at the Saigon guesthouse at about two in the afternoon.

Two or three weeks later we heard that there had been an attack on a convoy on that same road. Some were killed and several were wounded and captured. How long would we have to wait now for a convoy to Phnom Penh, Cambodia? Convoys were very unpredictable as to if and when they were going. All we could do was wait.

A week passed and still no scheduled convoy. I could sense that Merle was getting impatient. "Let's just trust the Lord and go on without a convoy," he finally suggested. The next day we were on our way alone with no earthly protection. The trip to Phnom Penh would take only a day *if* there were no delays. That was a big *if.*

Occasionally along the route, there was a military post or a guarded tower. Once, an army vehicle containing three soldiers passed us. Suddenly, one of them stood and pointed toward a certain field. We could see troops running to the area. They stopped and bent over a person or an object on the ground. After we passed the military vehicle, we came upon another one with large guns aimed at the field. Beyond that vehicle was still another one that appeared to have been fired at and damaged. Had we just missed an attempted ambush?

In front of us, a convoy of trucks coming down from Phnom Penh was being detained, but we were permitted to continue. Three days after we had traveled this road, the rebels cut a huge ditch across the road; it was a meter (39 inches) deep and 100 meters long, making travel impossible.

We finally arrived at a river that had to be crossed by ferry. A long line of traffic, including military vehicles, was waiting for a turn on the ferry. After a two-hour wait in the hot tropical sun, we were finally transported to the other side of the river. We were in Cambodia—our adopted homeland—and among the people whose congeniality would soon endear them to us.

After an enjoyable weekend in Phnom Penh, we prepared to leave for Battambang on Tuesday morning. "Why not stay one more day and rest before you go?" suggested our host and hostess, Floyd and Leanore Peterson.

"Thanks anyway," we replied. "We are anxious to reach Battambang and get settled again."

On the last day of January, a beautiful tropical morning with a cloudless blue sky, we drove through the countryside, admiring the lofty coconut trees and lovely sugar palms that graced the landscape. As we passed harvested rice fields and quiet little hamlets, we sang joyfully. With no convoy and no military posts along the way, we were alone in a strange land—or so we thought—and totally oblivious to the danger that could have been ours had we waited that one additional day in Phnom Penh. Only God Himself knew all the twists and turns our path would eventually take.

Soon after arriving in Battambang we heard the disturbing news: The day after we had left Phnom Penh, a band of rebels had barricaded that road from 11 a.m. until 4 p.m., looking for Frenchmen. A man of Swiss origin was taken captive into the woods and held for a few hours. He was eventually released when a Cambodian accompanying him pled on his behalf. The next day, a group of about 300 rebels stopped traffic for several hours on that same road. Had we been stopped during our journey, there would have been no way for us to communicate with the rebels. To do so in French might have meant death.

We did not know it then, but the day that we traveled to Battambang would be the last time that we dared risk taking that route for one full year. God's timing had been perfect. We had finally reached our destination in the intriguing land to which God had called us.

> You are my hiding place;
> > you will protect me from trouble
> > and surround me with songs of
> > > deliverance. (Psalm 32:7)

4

Lizards and Language

Cambodia was once the seat of a great and advanced empire that flourished from the ninth through the thirteenth centuries, encompassing vast surrounding territories in Southeast Asia and ruling over perhaps 60 million people. After the peripheral areas were lost to invading Siamese (Thai) and Vietnamese, France established a protectorate in 1863.

Approximately the size of the state of Missouri, Cambodia's territory is divided between mountain ranges and low-lying alluvial plains. Its shape has been likened to a flat bowl surrounded on three sides by mountains and on the fourth by the marshy delta of the Mekong River. The land is abundant in phosphates and, with well-watered, fertile soil, it is one of the richest rice-producing countries of the Orient. More than half of the country is carpeted with open woodlands or rain forests. The climate is tropical, divided between a wet season running from May to October and a dry season running from October until the following May.[1]

Physically, native Cambodians are small in stature, with bronzed skin. Most are rice farmers, fishermen or craftsmen.[2] Khmer is the dominant language, with Vietnamese and Chinese also used in the marketplace. Even though Cambodians dwell as neighbors to the Vietnamese, their characteristics, dress, customs, language and habits are entirely different.

The city of Battambang (or Batdambang), meaning "lost stick," is approximately 180 miles northwest of Phnom Penh toward the Thai border. Situated along the Sangke River, also referred to as the Battambang River, it is the market center for a fertile rice-growing region, and there is a substantial Chinese trading community with rice mills and other businesses. As Cambodia's second largest urban area, Battambang had a population of approximately 50,000-60,000 during the time we lived there.

The Alliance mission compound was situated in a community across the river from the market area. We were welcomed by Harold and Marguerite Sechrist, senior missionaries in charge of that district. A Cambodian neighbor, learning that we had arrived, came over the same afternoon to meet the new American lady and her little blonde-haired daughter. She talked to me, possibly about me, and felt our light skin, but all I could do was greet her with folded hands, a slight bow and a smile.

Behind the mission house was a former Bible school dormitory. Since the Bible school had been relocated to the Phnom Penh area, this vacant building would become our first Cambodian home. Constructed of bamboo, it sat on pillars about seven feet off the ground. The walls had been plastered both inside and out and then calcimined.

This reminds me of a barn, I thought as I ascended the steps to the living quarters of my new home and glanced around. The floors were made of rough, uneven boards that creaked when we walked, and an open space existed between the ceilings and walls throughout the building. There were no glass panes, bars or screens to grace the openings that served as windows, only unlouvered wooden shutters which were closed at night to discourage—and hopefully thwart—thieves. Merle eventually installed screens on the bedroom windows so we could leave them open to catch the evening breeze.

The building was divided into five rooms and a bathroom. I walked to the kitchen. It was totally bare except for built-in grates to use in cooking over charcoal. There were no cupboards, no workspace, no sink or running water. Where was I to put my pots and pans and prepare meals? We finally found an old table, painted it and brought it to the kitchen for a work area. A few boards nailed together provided shelves for the pots and pans. A refrigerator crate served first as a clothes closet and later as a cupboard in the kitchen.

Along the riverbank in front of the mission house, many people lived in houseboats. There they bathed, washed their clothes, dumped their garbage and drank the water. Thankfully, our water was carried from the river or from a city faucet up numerous narrow steps to the kitchen. A large, wide-mouthed clay water pot was placed in the kitchen to store water for use there, and another one was placed in the bathroom.

Water was also poured into a cement vat outside the house, where it was settled with alum and then pumped into a tank placed near the roof. From there it ran through a pipe to the shower area and then emptied via a piece of bamboo through a hole in the wall to the yard below. The drinking water and the water used for cooking had to be filtered through cotton, then boiled for twenty minutes. Our clothes were all laundered by hand in the river water, the white articles and linens first being boiled.

The building had been vacant for several months, and we found that it housed many unwelcome occupants—cockroaches, ants, mice, spiders and silverfish. Dozens of cockroaches, many huge and with wings, invaded our kitchen at night. It was necessary to keep food either in the refrigerator or in a screened cupboard with each leg sitting in a dish filled with creosote to discourage infestation. Insects ate holes in the living room curtains, and little lizards ran over our walls. A friendly gecko perched on Marilyn's bedroom wall, appearing at times to be watching her and entertaining us with his seven *tokays*.

I still remember my encounter with a large mouse that had been feasting on our bananas. I walked into the kitchen one evening and saw the mouse sitting on the table by the window. Since it made no effort to move, I ventured to hit it with my bare hand. As it started to run, I delivered a harder blow and knocked it out of the window to the ground below.

After we were settled in our new home, it was time to begin Cambodian language study. *Kaw, khaw, ko, kho, ngo.* Each day we repeated over and over the

Cambodian alphabet, which consists of thirty-three consonants and twenty-one vowels. There are also twelve unmodified sounds, eight accent and special marks, and ten numerals. Since the characters can be placed above or below, as well as following each other, and there is no space between words, we had our work cut out for us. Our teacher was a former Buddhist monk who had professed to accept Christ. He could speak neither French nor English, and it was therefore sometimes very difficult for us to grasp the meaning of abstract words.

Study time in the evenings was about the same time that hordes of mosquitoes invaded the house. I once counted forty bites on my legs. With wide-open windows and no screens except in the bedrooms, the building literally swarmed with flying creatures as we sat trying to absorb what we had studied that day.

It was necessary to hire household help, but initially we could not communicate with them. Can you imagine attempting to train a cook who not only did not understand what I was saying (and vice versa) but who also had no particular expertise as a chef? We cooked and baked over charcoal. There were no fast foods or mixes available; everything was made from scratch. We ground our own meat and made our own bread, using a starter in the absence of yeast. Flour was usually full of weevils, and we had to sift it through two different sieves.

I had brought a few packages of gelatin powder with me from the States. Before leaving for class on my first day of study, I watched the cook stir up a batch and set it aside. Using "sign language," I attempted to instruct him on how to prepare our lunch. It included frying some bacon. When I returned at noon, the bacon was nowhere to be seen. I concluded that he had forgotten to fry it. To my amazement, it soon became clear that he had cut up the raw bacon and put it in the JELL-O!

Another young man who was from the country was helping with the laundry and ironing on a table under the house. "That Mrs. must have a good iron," he told another Cambodian. "I have dropped it two or three times, and it still works."

There were times when I laughed at my own mistakes also. I finally changed cooks and hired a young married woman who was a Christian. Since she could read Cambodian, I could just give her recipes. One afternoon I asked her, so I thought, to boil two eggs as part of the evening menu. When we arrived at the table, there were two small boiled tomatoes instead.

"Where are the eggs?" I asked.

"You didn't ask me to boil eggs. You told me to boil tomatoes," she replied.

One of our most frustrating experiences as new missionaries later became legendary in our family. We jokingly referred to it as "The Day that Merle Held Up the Train."

"I'll take the suitcases to the train station while you finish your work and get ready," said Merle early that February morning.

Harold and Marguerite Sechrist, their little daughter and we three were leaving for the annual Cambodian National Church Conference to be held on the

Bible school compound near Phnom Penh. We were taking the train because the road to Phnom Penh was still too dangerous to travel by car. Buses were being stopped and passengers robbed. Occasionally, someone was taken and held for ransom. One truck approaching a guerrilla band was ordered to stop, and when the driver did not stop as quickly as the rebels desired, they fired, killing one or two occupants.

I was busy defrosting the refrigerator and doing last-minute tasks before we left. The electricity was erratic and unpredictable, which always necessitated our turning the refrigerator off when we left town for a period of time.

As I walked into the living room, I noticed Merle's briefcase sitting on the floor. Unaware that he planned to take it with him, I picked it up and put it on top of the desk. When he returned from the station, I called for him to bar the back door and close the kitchen shutters. With all supposedly secure and in order, we climbed into a *remorque* (a two-wheeled vehicle pulled by a bicycle) and took off for the train station.

Once we were on our way, I thought I had better check to see if Merle had heard me ask him to close the kitchen shutters. "I didn't hear you tell me to do that," he replied.

For a moment everything was silent. "What should we do?" I asked. "Someone could easily climb in and steal everything."

"Too late now," replied Merle.

When we arrived at the depot, Merle noticed that his briefcase was missing. Because I had moved it, he had not seen it as he left the house. His camera, our passports and other important documents were all in it. What were we to do? The train was due to leave in just a few minutes, and, to make matters worse, we lived on the other side of the river.

"Harold, can you go and ask the conductor if I have time to go back to the house?" asked Merle.

"There is no possible chance that you can make it."

"But I've got to have it," pled Merle. "All our official documents are in it."

"You go and try asking him," I told Merle, hoping to ease the tension.

We had been in Battambang less than a month and could not yet sufficiently communicate in the Khmer language. Merle talked to the conductor in French and, having received a favorable reply, sped off in a *remorque*, calling to the driver, "Hurry, hurry!"

When they came to the bridge spanning the river, to the amusement of bystanders, Merle jumped out and pushed the *remorque* from behind to help the driver go faster over the creaky wooden boards. He was running against time. Once home, Merle closed the shutters, grabbed the briefcase and started back.

Meanwhile, Marilyn and I had boarded the train with the Sechrist family. I stood at the window anxiously watching for his return, a myriad of thoughts racing through my mind: *What if the train leaves without him, and I am on board without any money or travel documents? What if he doesn't make this train? There is only one train a day and even that schedule is unpredictable. What will he have to eat at home? I defrosted the refrigerator and gave away all the food.*

I prayed and watched as a parade of *remorques* came and went. Finally, I saw Merle coming. What a relief! As he stepped on board, the whistle blew and the train lurched out of the station.

On the train we shared a compartment with the Sechrists. There were two bench seats, one facing the other, hardly sufficient for six passengers plus provisions for the long, hot trip. I was wearing a new cotton dress that I had saved for this occasion. En route, a spark from the engine blew in the open window and burned a hole in my dress.

Since there was always imminent danger of a possible rebel ambush along the way, the train had one armored car with soldiers perched on top, watchful and ready to deal with any such emergency. Sometimes mines were placed on the tracks. We passed by train stations that had been burned, evidence of previous attacks. Inside the passenger cars, armed soldiers walked up and down the aisles. Each Frenchman on board carried a gun. Even a French lady walked by us with a gun on her shoulder. It was an unsettling experience, but we were taking refuge in the promises of God: "The LORD will keep you from all harm—/ he will watch over your life;/ the LORD will watch over your coming and going/ both now and forevermore" (Psalm 121:7-8).

We finally arrived in Phnom Penh at 6 o'clock that evening, weary but thankful that the Lord had indeed watched over our comings—and particularly our goings.

Notes

1. Information gathered from the *Encyclopedia Americana International Edition*, 2001 ed., vol. 16, pages 273-274.
2. Ibid.

5

Under His Wings

The Issaraks, an anti-French nationalist group, were very active in the Battambang Province. Whether through raids at night or encounters by day, roving bands caused fear and anxiety among the people and made travel risky and dangerous.

We had been in Cambodia for less than three months when it became necessary for us to return to Dalat, Vietnam, for the annual Field Forum. But by what means could we possibly get out of Battambang? Air service had been suspended, and the road to Phnom Penh remained too dangerous to travel by car. We were warned that going by train meant we might have to spend a night en route if the train could not complete the journey in one day.

Harold enquired concerning the possibility of driving north to Sisophon, then southeast to Siem Reap, and from there down to Phnom Penh. He was informed that two convoys a month, if we were lucky, went from the town of Sisophon, traveling approximately thirty-five miles through the guerrilla-infested territory, and that the schedule was unpredictable.

One Wednesday Harold came to our home and announced, "I have heard that a convoy is going Friday. Be prepared to leave that morning." Only one day in which to wash, iron, pack suitcases and complete all other necessary tasks? Because of rebel activity in the area, it was not wise to burn lights late at night. How could I possibly make it? Nevertheless, we managed to get everything together and packed for the trip.

It was April, one of the hottest months of the year and still the dry season; there had been only an occasional afternoon shower. Merle decided to pray for rain to settle the dust on the road. On Friday morning, as we formed our caravan of two vehicles, it began to pour. How much more pleasant that would make the trip!

As we drove into Sisophon, we saw no sign of a convoy. "I didn't tell you," Merle said, "but yesterday, Harold learned that there would possibly not be a convoy after all. They suggested we could still make the trip if there were two or three cars traveling together."

There was no turning back now. Leaving Sisophon, Harold took the lead; he was followed by our car and, last of all, by a vehicle driven by a Cambodian businessman from Battambang. Harold flew a small American flag on his car. We were not sure that it would provide any security.

A long stretch of the road to Siem Reap was gravel. With the hot tropical sun beating down on us we kept our car windows wide open, and the dust ascended on us in billows, permeating every inch of the car and coating our bodies as well as our baggage.

Before we had reached the town of Siem Reap, our little Renault developed trouble. When Harold realized that we were missing from the convoy, he turned and came back. Our radiator was dry. Emptying our thermos and part of Harold's, we were finally able to proceed on to Siem Reap where we planned to stay overnight with missionaries Joe and Paula Doty.

After careful inspection, the men found that the rough road had caused the radiator to be partially torn from the car. There were no garages in town, so Merle and Harold began the task of removing the radiator in the hope that they could find someone who could solder it. About that time, Joe's landlord, a very wealthy Cambodian who operated a bus route out of Siem Reap, walked into the yard. "What are you doing?" he asked after the usual greetings. "I will send one of my mechanics over." How wonderfully the Lord had answered prayer!

The following day we visited the famous ruins of Angkor Wat and Angkor Thom. The word *angkor* derives from the Sanskrit word for "capital city." Geographically, it denotes seventy-five or more square miles of fertile plain where, between the ninth and thirteenth centuries AD, a dozen Khmer kings constructed their successive capitals. That culture eventually died, and the people who built the impressive Angkor edifices disappeared, leaving the story of their past carved in the beautiful laterite, sandstone and bricks. For centuries the monuments lay overgrown and unnoticed until they were finally discovered and rescued from the jungle. The whole complex of temples, monuments and irrigation systems makes the site one of the architectural wonders of the world.[1]

Angkor Wat, or "temple," is the largest and most famous of the monuments. Built with a series of rectangular walls surrounding an interior temple, it is breathtaking both in size and in artistic accomplishment. Along its walls, sculptures in bas-relief unfold narratives of ceremonial events and military victories achieved by the Angkor kings. One section depicts the Cambodians' concept of heaven and hell, in which the torments of hell and fire are contrasted to the joys of heaven, where the saints are served and waited on.

We stood enraptured as we gazed at the sculptured history of a people whose memory was now entwined among the roots of trees and vines with only the musty smell of bats and the echoes of birds and monkeys for company. How was it possible that such heavy stones could have been carved and hauled from the mountains, lifted to such heights and fitted together so perfectly to form these mammoth structures? Through the centuries, this place had stood silently, not giving up the secret and mystery of the people who had built and occupied it.

The steps leading up to the inner temple were so steep that I looked up in awe, wondering whether or not to attempt them. As we looked upon that place, we were impressed with the utter helplessness and hopelessness of the Buddhist religion. Idols—broken idols, dusty idols and stumps of idols minus heads, arms and legs—could be seen everywhere. Offerings were being made and incense sticks were being burned.

There were images of Buddha in various pos-
tures; one showed him sitting on a snake that was
overshadowing him. The legend goes that one time
when Buddha sat down, a snake coiled over him to
protect him and give him shade. His sitting on the
snake is said to indicate that Buddha was the victor.
However, the snake coiling over him only illus-
trated for us the fact that he was under the power of
Satan.

One area of the site was called "The Place of the
Thousand Gods." An old Cambodian woman sat at
the place of offerings. We found out that she had
cared for this place for twenty years. When Harold
witnessed to her concerning the Lord Jesus, she replied, "We cannot throw away these gods. They are
the gods of our ancestors. You say my god is dead.
Where is your God?"

That question continued to ring in my ears: "Where
is your God?" I thought of the picture so vividly described in Psalm 115:2-8:

> Why do the nations say,
>   "Where is their God?"
> Our God is in heaven;
>   he does whatever pleases him.
> But their idols are silver and gold,
>   made by the hands of men.
> They have mouths, but cannot speak,
>   eyes, but they cannot see;
> they have ears, but cannot hear,
>   noses, but they cannot smell;
> they have hands, but cannot feel,
>   feet, but they cannot walk;
>   nor can they utter a sound with their throats.

> Those who make them will be like them,
> and so will all who trust in them.

Leaving Siem Reap on Monday morning, we soon discovered that our radiator was still leaking. Unfortunately, whoever had soldered it had not found all of the holes. That meant that we had to stop every twelve to twenty miles to add water, and the leak was becoming progressively worse. It was also becoming increasingly difficult for us to find water. The only solution was for us to be towed. Thankfully, we had a rope, so for the rest of the journey to Phnom Penh—more than 100 miles—Harold towed us.

Then, as we were entering an area where the Issaraks were known to be active, Harold's tire went flat. While the men repaired it, Marguerite and I anxiously scanned the open fields for possible signs of a guerrilla band.

With the repaired tire finally in place, we proceeded on our way, but another crisis was about to take place—Harold, still with our vehicle in tow, hit a pig. When it came rolling toward us, Merle braked and swerved, causing the tow rope to snap. Another stop, this time to repair the rope.

Along the way there were other occasional detours. One of them took us for some distance through a field where the dust was more than ankle deep. It rose up in clouds, blowing into our faces, filling our nostrils, covering the windshield and making it difficult for us to see ahead even as far ahead as the Sechrist's car. We decided to roll up the windows, which caused us to perspire even more profusely, resulting in a mixture of dust and perspiration running like muddy water down our faces and arms.

After more than 9 hours and 190 miles, we finally arrived at the missionary guesthome in Phnom Penh and were able to continue our journey to Dalat for the Field Forum.

After the forum, we prepared to head for home. We left Dalat and flew to Saigon on Tuesday; then it was on to Phnom Penh on Thursday. While in Phnom Penh we learned that the situation in Cambodia had not improved. A few days after we had left Battambang, mortar shells had torn up the new airstrip, and some areas of the main highway were still being controlled by the Issaraks. Several bridges had been destroyed, and train tracks were being torn up in various places. One train had been derailed; a few cars had been overturned, and approximately ten people were killed.

Later that weekend, while we were still in Phnom Penh, we heard disturbing news: A bus had been stopped and passengers robbed in an area through which we would be traveling. We planned to leave for Battambang on Tuesday, but on Monday I became ill with fever, and we were unable to leave on schedule. Who knows? Perhaps it was in the providence of God that we did not travel that day.

We finally left Phnom Penh on Wednesday, and we encountered no difficulty on the Phnom Penh/ Siem Reap road except that the radiator in our car was showing continued signs of wear. Since it was not yet leaking, we decided to proceed. We were in the lead, with Harold and Marguerite following. After passing the village of Kralanh, Harold pulled up beside us and called, "Just ahead at the wooded mountain is where I believe that the bus was stopped. Go through as fast as you can." Yet even as he spoke, Harold's car suddenly stopped. Efforts to get it started failed. We were stranded in one of the most dangerous areas in all of Cambodia!

Finally, we saw a vehicle approaching. It was a truck that had come from Battambang and the only vehicle we saw on that particular stretch of road. The occupants of the truck informed us that they had encountered no problems on the road. They stayed with us until Harold's car eventually started and we took off. Twice we passed the mountain, and twice we turned back to search for Harold. Each time we found him at practically the same place, having made little if any progress.

"You try to pull me this time," said Harold.

We tried for a distance, but it proved impossible for our little loaded Renault to pull Harold's loaded Ford. The next town, Sisophon, was still twenty-five miles away.

"Leave your baggage here with me," suggested Harold. "Take my family and go to Sisophon for help."

We had no assurance, of course, that immediate help would be available, and darkness would soon be falling. We could not leave Harold alone in that dangerous and precarious situation. Even if help arrived, it would be even more risky to travel at night.

Harold decided to start the motor once more, but first he asked Merle to pray. On the next try, the motor turned and started. Harold now took the lead, and we moved—very slowly at times—until we reached Sisophon.

Merle pulled alongside Harold and called, "Shall we go on?"

Harold was hoping to arrive home before nightfall, and fearing to stop lest his car not start again, he replied, "I'm praying all the way."

At 6:15 p.m. we finally arrived in Battambang. The journey would be forever etched in our minds. God had been good to us—He had once again watched over our comings and goings.

Upon our return we found our house to be filled with spider webs and dust. The soiled clothes that I had left behind smelled musty, and the bed linens had begun to mildew. The man in charge of laundry was ill with the mumps and was unable to work for another week. But we had survived the trip, and that was all that mattered right then.

"What's that noise?" I sat bolt upright in bed. It was 2 a.m. The double door at the bottom of the steps leading up to our living room was shaking as though someone were trying to force it open. The door was so unstable that we placed an iron bar across the inside of it at night—but could it be broken open anyway? We had heard stories about robberies and, occasionally, kidnappings taking place on our side of the river. Had the Issarak rebels finally come for us?

Earlier that night, around midnight, gunfire had erupted, and Merle and I had sat at the foot of Marilyn's bed for a long time. I finally returned to bed and, just as Merle was returning, there was this new noise. I crawled out from under the mosquito netting, and together we tiptoed back into Marilyn's bedroom lest creaky boards reveal our location.

"Maybe I should go for my gun," Merle whispered. After a moment of silence, he said, "No, I have come here to bring peace."

We waited and prayed. All became quiet, and we returned to bed once more. We never did find out who or what was shaking our door.

There were two Buddhist temples on our side of the river, one just down the road beyond the mission property and another one a short distance in the opposite direction. One evening the guerrillas robbed the temple just beyond us. Then, apparently learning that the French police commissioner had gone to the temple to investigate the robbery, the guerrillas hid under the mission house to ambush the Frenchman and those accompanying him.

Harold and Marguerite came home from a church service and walked into the house shortly before the shooting began, unaware that guerrillas were hiding there. With window shutters open, Harold sat down to do some typing. Suddenly, gunfire erupted. As bullets began to fly, soldiers from across the river also opened fire. Fortunately, no one was killed and only a few were wounded, and thankfully, Harold and Marguerite were unharmed. The guerrillas then boasted in one of the villages that they had hidden under the mission house.

Being the senior missionary on the station, Harold was concerned about our safety at night. Behind the mission property were open fields through which the Issaraks could move freely since there was no adequate security on our side of the river. Harold insisted that we must sleep at their house each night. We fixed up a small room leading off their back porch as a bedroom for ourselves. The room itself was actually no safer than our house, but, if and when shooting began, we were to dash into the main brick section of the Sechrists' house.

The governor of the province was also concerned about us. He offered to send soldiers to guard our property at night. We all preferred that they did not come lest it only increase the risk of danger. He sent them anyway, and their presence became evident in more ways than one. We had purchased twenty chickens in order to have fresh eggs, and each morning after the soldiers went off duty, another chicken would be missing. This continued until all the chickens had been stolen.

Regardless of our circumstances, we claimed God's promise in Psalm 91:4:

> He will cover you with his feathers,
> and under his wings you will find refuge;
> his faithfulness will be your shield and rampart.

Note

1. This information is compiled from the author's experience
   and from information found in *The National Geographic*, Vol.
   161, number 5, May 1982.

6

Good News from Heaven

The original plan had been for us to move to Kompong Chhnang when housing became available. There had never been a resident missionary in that province, and we were looking forward to opening a new station there. However, while we were still in our first year of language study, Harold and Marguerite Sechrist were transferred to Bible school ministry near Phnom Penh, and we were appointed to replace them in Battambang.

We would be overseeing a large district made up of two provinces, Battambang and Pursat. Battambang was the second oldest mission station in Cambodia, having been opened by David and Muriel Ellison in 1923. It was the home of the only church building at that time and also had the largest number of outstations and Christians in residence. We would be responsible for an area approximately 150 miles by 80 miles, with over 450,000 inhabitants.

The countryside had a particular beauty of its own. In the growing season, the paddies stretched emerald green with transplanted rice and later teemed with golden grain. Sugar palms, the national tree, grew in abundance. Their leaves served as roofs over the houses of the poor, their fruit was very palatable, and their juice was extracted to make sugar.

The local farmers lived in small groupings or villages composed of 20 to 100 houses built on stilts and entered by a ladder with an uneven number of steps (a matter of superstition). Because of the stilts, the houses were above the level of the flood waters, were provided good air circulation, had better protection from pests and rats and afforded an open storage area for farming implements. The houses of the wealthy farmers were constructed of wood and had tile roofs, while those of the poor were made of woven palm or coconut tree leaves plaited on bamboo lattices.

There were two kinds of farmers: the rice-paddy farmers and the riverside farmers. During its flood season, the Mekong River carried fresh soil which, after the waters had subsided, was left along the riverbanks. This soil was very fertile and nurtured a variety of crops such as soy beans, jute, cotton, corn and other vegetables. While the rice-paddy farmer had only one harvest each year, the riverside farmer had two—one during the dry season when his land was still moist and another during the rainy season.

Along the road in Battambang one might encounter a farmer transporting his harvest to market in a creaking oxcart, a wooden box placed on a frame with four-and-a-half-foot wheels and pulled by two oxen. Or one might hear the shrill squeal of a pig as it was taken to market tied onto the back of a bicycle. Young lads could be seen herding water buffalo, catching crabs in watery fields or splashing in muddy pools.

In the villages, however, the people devoted their working hours and their spare time to numerous small industries: the manufacture of bronze bowls, axes, ploughs, sickles, earthenware stoves, woven cane mats and rattan baskets.

The traditional costume of the Cambodian woman was a blouse and a *sampot,* which was an ankle-length skirt made of a single piece of fabric wrapped around the waist and overlapped in the front. A dark color was normally worn for daily activities, but a richly colored *sampot* was donned on feast days. The masculine version of the *sampot* was the sarong, but men in town normally wore European dress.

The Buddhist temple was the center of social life for the Cambodians. Even the smaller villages had at least one temple. Beautiful pagodas crowned with their many pointed, multi-colored roofs were sacrificially kept by the people. Encompassing the temples stood *stoupas,* small structures built on the temple grounds where the ashes of the deceased were kept. Within the temple grounds were the monastic dwellings, wooden buildings with tile roofs, which were occupied by the monks.

It was customary for at least one son in every family to enter the priesthood, if only for a short time, thereby attaining merit for himself and for his family. In the early morning, these saffron-robed monks went out in single file to beg for their food. The villagers placed rice in their begging bowls, which were carried suspended from a shoulder strap. The monks had to return to the pagoda before noon to partake of their single meal. Only liquid refreshment was permitted after midday. The monks made themselves available for regular merit-making ceremonies for the common people, and their monotonous chanting could be heard at many events.

Musicians were often hired for important occasions such as weddings, funerals, parades and religious ceremonies that were held to earn merit for the dead. Following the lead of one instrument, the musicians could play for hours or even days with few pauses. It was literally possible to go to sleep with the repetitious tune of one of those orchestras ringing in one's ears and awaken the next morning to the same tune. Sometimes a public-address system made the blast of music even more wearisome.

Occasionally interspersed in the monotonous music was the sad, plaintive tone of a flute-like instrument playing in a minor key and coupled with an intermittent drumbeat. Then we knew that a corpse was on its way to the temple grounds to await cremation. Another soul had gone into a Christless eternity.

Not long after we moved into the mission house, a wedding was held at the home of a wealthy neighbor. Cambodian custom dictated that marriages were to be arranged by the families involved. To officially ask for the hand of a young woman in marriage, the parents and relatives of the suitor, accompanied by intermediaries and friends, go with great pomp and many presents to the house of the girl's parents, who officially accept the offer of marriage. Together with the parents of the young man, who defray all the costs, the

girl's parents arrange the details of the marriage cere-
mony and feast, which are to take place at the home of
the young bride. After the wedding, at which monks
chant and give their blessing, the bride changes into a
beautiful costume. Then she and the groom greet
those who are seated at the feast.

When we attended our neighbor's wedding feast, I
was unaware that all of the other guests to be seated
and served would be men, so I felt a bit out of place
when I discovered that I was the only woman being
served.

Wrapped presents were not brought to the feast.
Rather, money was placed in an envelope and added
to a contribution that would be presented later to
the married couple.

One day a Cambodian from one of the outlying
villages presented us with an unusual pet—a mon-
key. We called her Dopey, though the name did not
really befit her disposition, as she was very intelligent
and mischievous. We kept her leashed to the railing
of our back porch. Eventually she discovered that
her leash would reach to the office window, and one
day she reached through the bars and knocked over a
bottle of ink on the desk. At the sight of a baby, she
would make gestures indicating that she wanted to
hold one also. I was concerned that Dopey might
break her leash, get into the house and wreak havoc.

One day we realized that Dopey was missing. Having finally freed herself from the leash, she had made
her way to the home of a neighbor, found their money

jar and scattered the contents. After all her other an-
tics, that was the final straw. It was time for Dopey to
have a new home, and we gave her away to a Cambodian living in the area.

Located on the mission property in Battambang
was a children's hostel. Since children in the small
villages at that time had to attend Buddhist schools
if they desired an education, David Ellison had established the hostel in 1947. It provided a place for
the children to stay while attending the city schools.
Normally the house was full, but at that time, with
the unsettled conditions in the district, it was at
about half its former occupancy.

Most of the children who came to the house were
from Christian homes. The missionaries desired to
create a homelike, Christian atmosphere in which
the children would be strengthened in the faith or, if
they did not know Christ, be led into a personal relationship with Him. The children regularly attended
Sunday services and other scheduled meetings. It
was hoped that from these children would come future Bible school students and leaders of the Cambodian Church.

One of our first concerns when we settled into our
home was finding a pastor to reach the Chinese population in the city. Samuel Mok, a young Chinese
man who was a recent graduate of the Bible school
in Hong Kong, came to live on our compound. He
had answered the call of God to be a missionary
among the Chinese in Cambodia.

Realizing his talents, the communists in China had wanted Samuel to work for them, but he had refused. "I believe in God, and He has called me to preach," he told them.

They threatened him by putting a revolver to his heart. "Join us or we will kill you," they said.

"Go ahead," replied Samuel. "I'll be with Jesus. He lives in my heart."

One of the communists drew a knife. "We'll cut out your heart and see if He lives there," he said.

"You won't see Him," replied Samuel, "because you cannot see Him with physical eyes. You can only see Him with the spiritual."

They put him in prison and attempted to starve him, but other prisoners secretly shared their meager portions sufficiently for Samuel to stay alive. At last he was told, "We will let you go if you promise to never preach on Genesis chapter one."

"I cannot promise," Samuel said. "I must preach the whole Bible."

Samuel would not yield, and he was eventually released. After graduation from Bible school in Hong Kong, he came to Battambang. Though he did not speak the dialect that most of the Chinese there spoke, he began learning it and faithfully served as a pastor at the church he planted in Battambang until he was forced to leave just before the fall of the country to communism. At that point there were two Cambodian services and two Chinese services each Sunday, in addition to Sunday school and weekly prayer meetings.

Also living on the mission compound was a wrinkled old Cambodian woman who occupied a small room in the hostel. After having accepted Christ as her Savior, she was ostracized by her family, so the mission granted permission for her to live on the compound. One day the woman fell ill, and the sickness appeared to be terminal. Since there would have to be an immediate burial in such a hot climate, a wooden coffin was made and stored in our garage.

Cambodians are normally cremated. With two temples near our home, we frequently smelled the sweetly sickening odor of burning flesh as the night breezes wafted it in our direction. However, the Cambodian Christians buried their dead, and this old woman was to be interred in a back section of the mission property.

The woman eventually died, and a grave was dug. But, since it was the rainy season and the ground was saturated, water began immediately to seep into the hole. The coffin, with a bamboo slat bottom, was the type regularly used for cremation. The Christians placed a mat in the bottom of the coffin and carefully laid the old woman inside. As it was lowered into the grave, I could picture her floating in water inside the coffin.

If I had any culture shock as a young missionary, this was it. I thought of the luxurious burials we had back home. But as we stood around the grave singing hymns of faith and hope, I praised the Lord that the woman's spirit had gone to be with Him. There would be no more weary and lonely days in a small, hot and bare hostel room. She was no longer a pauper, but an heir of God with a mansion in glory.

Ever since we had begun work in the district, political conditions had prevented us from traveling in many areas. Merle, in consultation with the local pastor, studied a map of the region and found that there were many villages still awaiting the message of salvation. The Lord protected him as he went, oftentimes at considerable risk, to some villages that no one had been able to visit since World War II, and to others where the gospel message had never been proclaimed. One of those trips was a never-to-be-forgotten experience, as we indicated in the following letter that we wrote to some friends of ours:

> We (Merle and two or three nationals) left Battambang about 7 o'clock in the morning and headed for a village where no missionary or national worker had visited for several years. We came to a road which led off of the main highway and inquired from some farmers nearby if this was the proper way to the village. No car had been over that road for the past year. Without any bridges and with tall field grass, it was now used only as an oxcart trail. It took us over an hour to go about twelve miles.
>
> Upon arriving at the village, we set up our public-address system, which was portable and run from the car battery. Quite a few people gathered. In addition to our witnessing and selling books, a Bible school student presented a flannelgraph lesson.
>
> We assumed that we could find an eating place in the village, but discovered that there

were none. A Chinese school teacher, seeing our plight, invited us to eat with him. Then rushing off, he hurriedly killed a chicken and prepared dinner.

After the meal, we started on our way again by another road. The dust was so thick that the inside of the car was completely covered. Observing a small village with a number of houses along the road, we stopped. But where were the people? No one appeared.

Once again we set up the public address system and began to play music. Out of the houses men, women and children began to pour until they were coming up the road, down the road and from every direction. Approximately 200 people listened attentively to the story of Jesus.

"We haven't seen a white man for a number of years," they said. "Please stay longer and tell us more."

But we had to leave since we were expected at another village farther on for an evening service. We started home about 7 o'clock. For the last thirty or more miles, we didn't see another car since no one traveled after dark because of the rebel activity. We arrived home after 8 p.m., rejoicing that some had been able to hear the story of Jesus for the first time.

There were many places, however, where it was utterly impossible for us to go. We had received authorization from the governor of the province to preach anywhere that we desired, as well as permission to hold open-air meetings in the town of Battambang. But when guerrilla activity was intense in a particular area, the people would be reluctant to receive gospel literature. If a missionary came for a service during the day, rebels would come that night and threaten or punish the Cambodian Christians. Out of fear, the Christians would then request that the missionary not come back until the area was more peaceful.

How could we reach some of those villages still awaiting the message of salvation? An idea was conceived: Why not sow the seed by air?[1]

Of course, there were problems with implementing such a project. How could it be done? Would this Buddhist government permit us to drop literature, especially in light of political conditions? Would the people in isolated areas be afraid to pick up the tracts, keep them and read them? But God, with whom nothing is impossible, provided us with a wide-open door.

Ed Roffe, a C&MA missionary in Laos, agreed to bring the mission plane down for this special task. Then the Lord burdened some of those in the homeland to pray and to give so that the Cambodian people might receive the Word of God.

When permission was sought from the governor of the province, he remarked, "I have never heard of anyone dropping this kind of literature by air; nevertheless, I do not see why it cannot be done." We were asked to give him a copy of each tract and gospel portion to be distributed and a list of all the towns over which we planned to fly. He planned to send the information to the king for approval.

In due time permission was granted. Then, before the literature could be dropped, a new governor came to the province. Happily, he also cooperated in every way. To our amazement, he even sent notices to all the villages that we had named, stating that on a certain day gospel portions pertaining to the Christian religion would be dropped and that the people should not be afraid to accept and read them. Moreover, he went along on the first trip and ordered twelve soldiers to guard the plane each night at the airfield.

Over the course of two days, approximately 16,000 tracts and 3,600 gospel portions were distributed in 45 villages, at least 38 of them receiving the good news for the first time. As the plane circled lower and lower and the literature was ejected, both yellow-robed monks and villagers could be seen running to receive a portion of God's Word. It was estimated that within those villages there were over 20,000 souls who could not be reached in any other way during that time.

There was one particular village, though, that either ignored the notice of the literature drop or never received it. Some time later, Merle met a French military officer who told him that soldiers in the area of that village had fired at an unrecognized plane dropping literature, perhaps assuming it to be propaganda. As they compared dates, they realized that it had been the mission plane. Neither Merle nor Ed had been aware of this incident, which could have easily resulted in tragedy. It was evidence once again of God's merciful protection.

Thirty miles down the winding river from Battambang was a village called "Old Forest." It was accessible only by boat. There were no roads or other means of entering, and no missionary or national worker had ever visited the village.

In this village lived a man named Yon. As Merle and Ed flew overhead and dropped portions of the Word of God, Yon picked up one tract titled "Ungratefulness." It contained the story of the prodigal son. The Spirit of God used these words to show Yon that he was like this wayward son who had wandered far from the bosom of his father. Yon himself was far away from God.

Several months later, we purchased some wood from a Vietnamese lady. She had bought it from a Cambodian man, who had brought it in by boat from a village downriver. Since the man had not measured the wood, the Vietnamese woman sent him to our compound to stack and measure it. This was how we met Yon. He told us his story and pulled the tract, now dirty and worn, from his pocket. Merle invited him to come to the house when his work was finished so he could hear more. Yon promised to do so.

That afternoon Yon went to the river, bathed, changed clothes and returned. He listened attentively for an hour to the story of God and His great plan of salvation. Then he prayed and accepted the Lord Jesus as his Savior. The next day he went back to his village, taking not only more of God's Word for himself but also some portions to give out to his friends.

One evening three weeks later, we returned home to hear the good news that Yon had returned to

Battambang and was waiting to see us. He informed us that his wife was now ready to believe as well. "She believes in her head already," he said. However, he wanted to bring her to the mission station so that she could pray and really accept the Lord into her heart.

We shall never know all of the harvest that may have been reaped from the seed that was sown in those days, but we have God's promise that "it will not return to [Him] empty,/ but will accomplish what [He] desire[s]/ and achieve the purpose for which [He] sent it" (Isaiah 55:11).

Note

1. See Merle Graven, "Sowing the Seed from the Air," *The Alliance Weekly*, August 13, 1952, n.p.

7

Because Someone Prayed

The missionary's lifeline is prayer. While we were in Cambodia, we depended unceasingly upon the faithfulness of those back home to lift us daily before the throne of God, and we often experienced the power of those prayers.

"Dear Lord, lay me upon the heart of someone back home today," I prayed one afternoon in July. I was going through a cycle of fever, sweat and chills. Every bone in my body seemed to be aching, especially my back. I was seven months pregnant.

Merle asked the French military doctor if he would come to the house to diagnose my problem. In the Orient, when there is a cycle of fever, perspiration and chills, malaria is immediately suspected, so the doctor suggested that I take quinine. However, I chose not to take the quinine for fear that it might affect my pregnancy. My suffering increased, and I began to worry. What if labor pains began? I was a day's journey by train to the hospital in Phnom Penh.

I asked Merle to anoint me with oil and pray for my deliverance. That night the cycle of fever and chills broke and my temperature dropped. Later, a rash appeared, which indicated that I had dengue fever, but I was on my way to recovery.

Then, while I was still weak and recuperating, Merle became ill with similar symptoms, though he didn't notice a rash. He developed complications that almost necessitated an emergency trip to Phnom Penh, but he also recovered.

It was a busy time for us. The date for our district conference was approaching, and the guest speaker would be staying with us. To add to the confusion, our Cambodian cook had been on maternity leave for almost three weeks. As the time approached for the birth of our baby, we had to make a decision: Would it be a day's journey by train to Phnom Penh or a trip to the border and a day's journey by train to Bangkok?

I chose to go to Bangkok, but to our dismay, a conflict developed between the Cambodian government and the Thai government and the border was closed. After much persuasion, we finally were granted special permission to cross the border.

The previous year Merle, Marilyn and I had gone to Bangkok by train for medical purposes, and the memory of that trip still lingered. It had been a four-hour train ride to the border town of Poipet. A young Cambodian man met us, asked for our passports and said that we would have to wait for two or three hours. However, a French immigration officer expedited our crossing by providing a truck to take us and our baggage directly to the customs official. From there we crossed the border to the Thai town of Aranyaprathet, proceeded through immigration and customs again and went on to the inn where we would stay for the night.

It became dark very early, around 6 o'clock. We had brought food for our lunch on the train, expecting to buy our evening meal in Aranyaprathet. But a stroll, cut short by threats of rain, produced nothing by way of a suitable eating place. So, Merle went to the market and bought some bananas. They would have to get us through until morning, and we would buy our lunch on the train the following day.

Our room at the inn was rather large, with two double beds. We let down the mosquito nets in order to spray them with the last remains of an insect bomb that we had brought with us, and hordes of mosquitoes flew in all directions. The beds were uncomfortable, each one with only one sheet that was too small to fit the hard mattress. Whenever we moved, the sheets moved with us.

When we went to pay for our room the following morning, the charge was double the price that the customs official had quoted to us the day before when he left us at the inn. When asked why the price had increased, the proprietor replied, "That included the luxuries and a double room." We were somewhat amused, wondering what he considered to be luxuries. Perhaps he meant the two spittoons, a pair of used thongs, a clay pot with water for the bathroom and a little round pan to use as a dipper, a small lamp and a bottle of water that we did not risk drinking.

When we boarded the train to Bangkok we found, to our chagrin, that the train had no diner. So at the first stop, Merle got off and purchased another cluster of bananas. We ate these together with the last scraps remaining from our lunch kit. The food I had originally packed for one meal had been stretched to four. Needless to say, it had not been an easy trip.

Marilyn would not be going with us on our second trip to Bangkok. She was away at boarding school in Dalat, Vietnam. With a heavy heart I had taken that last glimpse of her as the car proceeded down the driveway en route to the airport. Leaving a small child for the first time in another country was difficult. As a mother, I felt that no one would take care of her as I could. And then when Marilyn's first letter arrived, we learned that she had chicken pox!

On this second trip we asked one of the Christians to drive us to the border to make connection with the train, and all went well. But, while we were in Bangkok, I contracted a serious cold, was hospitalized for a few days and was given fourteen penicillin shots.

Fortunately, the baby was a bit late in arriving. In due time we welcomed into the family another lovely daughter, Ardelle Joanne. But the penicillin shots had affected my milk, and we were in danger of losing our precious gift before the cause of her problem was even discovered. The baby lost weight daily, and her bowels were affected. Medicine provided no help, so the doctor finally switched her to powdered milk, and Ardelle began to respond immediately. The problem had been caught just in time.

When we returned to Cambodia, the same Christian man met us at the border. As we drove the lonely, dark road, the car's headlights flickered and went out. Enveloped in inky blackness, we found our way by flashlight until we reached the next small village, where we were able to repair the lights sufficiently to get home.

Several months later, we faced a serious attack of malaria. "If I die . . ." Merle, although seriously ill, was giving me instructions for his burial in the event that he succumbed. He was perspiring so profusely that several sheets at a time were hanging in the tropical sun to dry.

As Merle's temperature continued to climb, he faced the possibility of delirium, and baby Ardelle and I were alone with him at the mission station. Our comfort in that hour was knowing that there were those in the homeland who cared for and prayed for us. The words that follow express our feelings in those dark days and on many other occasions:

> Because you prayed, someone in distant land
> Felt God reach down, extend His healing hand
> And bid affliction go at His command,
> Because you prayed.
>
> Because you prayed, someone across the sea
> Had strength renewed, sensed fear and anguish
>   flee;
> For God was there to give the victory,
> Because you prayed.[1]

An airline employee stood at our back door calling, "Mister, Mister!" It appeared to be the Cambodian custom to call at the door instead of knocking.

"We have no information that a plane will be coming today," he told us.

We were preparing to leave by plane to attend the Cambodian National Conference and then travel on to Dalat for our Field Forum. Commuter plane service between Phnom Penh and Battambang had been resumed ostensibly for twice-a-week flights—Tuesday and Friday—but the planes did not always arrive as scheduled.

Merle, Ardelle and I were booked on the Friday flight. Our suitcases had been packed in advance as much as possible, and we had wired the missionary in Phnom Penh to meet us at the airport. Now came the disappointing news that we might be delayed. Merle checked at the airline office that afternoon, but no word had yet been received. We sent another wire to Phnom Penh stating that we would not be coming that day.

On Saturday morning, Merle inquired further. Still no word concerning the plane. We bought food for the weekend and prepared to wait. After lunch we retired to the bedroom to take a brief siesta when, suddenly, we heard the motor of a plane overhead. Leaping out of bed, we ran to the back porch but could not identify the plane.

Merle rushed to the ticket office. The airline employees had seen the plane also, but it did not appear to be the commuter plane, and they had received no word that a plane was arriving that day. Feeling that he should check further, Merle drove to the airfield. There was a plane there! Guards informed him that it was a government plane that had come on an errand for the bank; the plane wasn't for us. How disappointing!

Later that day, at 1:30 p.m., we heard a voice at our back door again calling, "Mister, Mister!" A man from the ticket office was bringing news that the government plane would be leaving in half an hour and would take us to Phnom Penh. I overheard Merle say, "We'll be there."

Ready to leave in half an hour? I thought of all that had to be done and yelled, "I can't make it! I can't make it!"

The man promised that the plane would wait until 2:30. Merle repeated, "We'll be there."

I ran for the cook and asked her to hurriedly defrost the refrigerator and give away the food. The part-time *amah* was called to dress the baby; her husband would bring in the laundry and close the shutters. I hastily finished packing suitcases and got dressed. Merle ran up the road to the home of a wealthy Cambodian neighbor who had a jeep and asked if he could drive us to the airfield. We threw our suitcases into the jeep and departed.

There was only one other passenger on the plane with us. En route to Phnom Penh, I asked Merle, "How are we going to get from the airport to the missionary guesthome?"

"If the Lord has gotten us this far," Merle replied calmly, "He will get us the rest of the way."

As we arrived at the Phnom Penh airport, alighted from the plane and started walking toward the terminal building, the other passenger from the plane asked, "Do you have transportation into the city?"

"Not yet," Merle replied.

"You can come with me," he said. "I will have my chauffeur take you to your destination." He ordered soft drinks and invited us to be seated. We then learned that this man was an important government official who had gone to Battambang on an errand for the bank.

The Lord not only provided free transportation by plane to Phnom Penh, but we were also delivered directly to the gate of the missionary guesthome. Jehovah Jireh had truly been our provider that day.

"I plan to go to the village of Moung next Sunday," Merle announced one day.

There were a congregation of Christians and a pastor there, but Moung was situated about thirty miles south of Battambang on a road that had been too dangerous for us to attempt to travel for nearly two years.

Marilyn was home from Dalat School for vacation. I wanted to take her and fourteen-month-old Ardelle and go with Merle to Moung. "The way is dangerous," said Merle. "The tropical sun will be very hot for the children." Nevertheless, I decided that I should go.

It was the latter part of November, the end of the rainy season. The morning of our departure dawned bright and beautiful with the promise of a delightful tropical day. Normally, this would have been a pleasant trip, but things were not normal in Cambodia. The road was very rough and full of unrepaired potholes that were wide, deep and unavoidable. About halfway down the road was an area where guerrillas had frequently stopped buses and robbed passengers.

We had sold our little French Renault and had bought a used French Ford Vedette. As we approached the danger area, Merle said, "I am going to step on the gas and go by as fast as I can." Bouncing up and down over the isolated stretch of territory, we passed safely without encountering any difficulty or seeing any guerrillas.

That morning, Merle spoke to the adults at the worship service and I taught the children. The little chapel was filled to overflowing while others stood outside trying to see this white man who was speaking their language.

At the conclusion of the service, we started back to Battambang. All went well until we were approaching the danger spot. Once again Merle said, "I am going to step on the gas now." Suddenly, the car stopped dead. How could this happen? Why did our cars always seem to develop problems in the most dangerous areas?

Upon investigation Merle found that, due to the rough road, the bolts that attached the fuel pump to the motor had fallen off and were missing, causing the pump to flop up and down. We had seen no other vehicles on the road, and the probability of seeing anyone was about nil. Neither were there any inhabitants living nearby. The terrible truth was that we were in what appeared to be a no-man's land, stranded in guerrilla territory.

The hot tropical sun beat down upon us. It was approaching midday and the children were getting hungry and thirsty. Suddenly, Merle heard a whistle a short distance ahead. He looked around just in time to see a man carrying a gun jump down from some bushes onto the road. The man turned and motioned, and another man appeared, also carrying a gun. The two of them began marching toward our car. Because the hood was raised, I did not see them until they suddenly appeared by the side of the car. Merle ignored the visitors and continued searching for a bolt in the hopes that one had lodged somewhere in the car as it fell. The men stopped, watched for a while and then proceeded on their way down the road.

Finally, Merle found one bolt that held the fuel pump sufficiently until we arrived home. The men had not harmed us or even attempted to rob us. I recalled those promises from *Daily Light on the Daily Path* that God had given us that evening when we first arrived in Saigon. Once again, we had experienced the reality of His promise in Psalm 34:7:

> The angel of the LORD encamps
> around those who fear him,
> and he delivers them.

Note

1. Louisa Graven, Ft. Myers, FL, 1997.

8

Tears and Triumph

Although Merle was just thirty-two years old, his health had been steadily declining for several months. He had lost thirty-nine pounds, and his hair was fast turning gray. His illness had been diagnosed as amoebic dysentery. He had received treatment, but he had not improved.

The field executive committee was planning to meet in Phnom Penh. Since Merle was a member of the committee, he decided to chance going by train, although trains were still subject to attack by the Issarak rebels. Marilyn was back at the Dalat School, and Ardelle and I would remain in Battambang.

While in Phnom Penh, Merle went to the hospital to consult the French doctor there. After a chest Xray, the doctor said, "My equipment is old, but I believe that you have tuberculosis and should return to the United States immediately."

Merle was both shocked and grieved. As he later told me, he returned to the missionary guesthome and wept before the Lord. Imagine my great disappointment when Merle returned to Battambang and said that we must pack to leave immediately! Our home assignment was due in a few months, but Merle would be returning in broken health. What did the future hold?

Why, Lord? I thought of all the miracles that God had wrought to bring us to Cambodia and to protect us while we were there. Why would He permit us to labor there for only a short time? Though we did not understand what God desired to accomplish in our lives through these circumstances, we decided to trust Him to work out His sovereign purpose. We disposed of most of our possessions and sadly departed.

It Is Not Always Mine to Know

It is not always mine to know
Just why the Lord does lead me so;
But this I know, He doeth well
And someday when with Him I dwell,
I'll understand the path He chose
Was best for me. And as time goes
I learn to lean upon His Word,
And with His strength my loins I gird
That I might run the race to win,
And not be found with stain or sin;
And in each battle to be fought,
I'll trust in Him for He has wrought
Salvation full and free for me
Which guarantees the victory.
The future years I will not fear,
For He has promised to be near;
And, though the foe be sometimes strong
And trials seem so very long,
Yet He who goeth on before
Will lead the way to heaven's door.[1]

****

Back home in the United States, Merle and I, along with Marilyn and Ardelle, were now in need of another miracle. Merle underwent various physical tests; he did not have tuberculosis nor could the doctors find any trace of amoebic dysentery. The new diagnosis was a spastic intestine.

By the end of two years Merle had improved, but he could not obtain medical clearance to return to Cambodia. It would have been easy to think that God had closed the door. However, we both believed that our ministry in Cambodia was not finished. Merle wrote to our Division of Overseas Ministries (now called International Ministries). "I am willing to return to Cambodia and trust the Lord if you will grant permission and trust the Lord with us," he said. They granted permission. When we returned by faith, Merle experienced a miracle of healing from the Lord.

Upon our arrival in Phnom Penh, we were greeted by a tropical rain, which is typical for an afternoon in July. I had been assigned the responsibility of the mission guesthouse. Merle was business agent, had oversight of the Phnom Penh city work and was pastor of the International Church. This was an English-speaking congregation composed of embassy personnel, government workers, the US Military Aid Assistance Group and others. We met every Sunday morning at 11 o'clock in an air-conditioned chapel in the American Embassy building.

An International Exposition (Expo) was going to be held in Phnom Penh beginning November 15. Merle rented a booth to feature the new Cambodian Bible, distribute gospel literature and daily give forth the Word to thousands who might not otherwise hear it. The British and Foreign Bible Society was sharing in the expense, and national workers would be witnessing in three different languages—Cambodian, Vietnamese and Chinese. Merle applied for and received permission to use the public-address system and to hold outdoor rallies in the city. At night, colored slides on the life of Christ would occasionally be shown with story interpretation in the various languages. We were looking forward to this wonderful opportunity to sow the seed.

Then, in the midst of all the preparations, Merle became ill with a cold and flu-like symptoms. On Monday, November 14, the day before the Expo was to begin, one of Merle's knees hurt so badly that he went to the hospital to see the French doctor. He was running a fever and had a bronchial cough, and the bottom of both of his feet had begun to swell. The doctor ordered him to return home, go to bed and come back the following day for Xrays.

In the meantime, ten-year-old Marilyn had come home from school in Vietnam for vacation. She too began to complain of some pain and discomfort, first in the rib area and then in her back and chest. The problem developed further with a headache, dizziness, some stiffness and pain along the spinal area and a fever. Both Merle and Marilyn were anointed and prayed for that evening by Harold Sechrist and Rev. Curwen Smith, a C&MA missionary who was on loan to the British and Foreign Bible Society and was in Phnom Penh at that particular time. The following morning they went to the hospital, where the doctor diagnosed Merle's condition as circulatory rheumatism and Marilyn's as probable spinal meningitis.

"Take her home and bring her back at 3:30 this afternoon for a spinal tap," the doctor said. "We have no available room for her in the hospital now, but we will prepare one." I was astonished that a child so critically ill would be sent home. Partial paralysis in her neck and throat had already impaired Marilyn's speech.

That afternoon Marilyn's spine was tapped, and the doctor announced that she had a serious case of meningitis. "We will have to wait until morning to see if further paralysis will set in," he said.

Harold Sechrist, the field chairman, wired The Christian and Missionary Alliance headquarters in the States for special prayer. He also wired the mission in Saigon for a nurse and asked the mission secretary in Phnom Penh to temporarily assume my responsibilities in the guesthome.

Merle insisted on staying at the hospital with Marilyn the first night but became so ill that he had to return to bed the following day. Lois Chandler, the Dalat School nurse, had arrived in Saigon from home assignment and was asked to go immediately to Phnom Penh to assist with Marilyn. She and I took turns around the clock at the hospital. We shall be forever grateful for her faithful help at that time.

The first morning in the hospital, Marilyn was given only bread and black coffee for breakfast, so I asked permission to bring meals to her at the hospital. Traveling across town through a stream of traffic while endeavoring to transport hot food became a daily challenge.

A top specialist in the field of meningitis was in Phnom Penh at that time, and after consultation with the specialist, the attending physician, Dr. Riche, prescribed heavy doses of penicillin to be given to Marilyn intramuscularly, along with two kinds of vitamin B intramuscular shots, each day. To avoid the possibility of infection from improperly sterilized needles, Lois requested permission to give the shots herself. Marilyn had forty intramuscular shots in less than two weeks, and her screams grew louder as each day the shots became more painful to bear.

And then she suffered a reaction to the penicillin. Several cultures were taken, and the doctor ordered another spinal tap. Realizing how painful it would be for her, I wished that Merle could be there with us, but he was still bedfast at home. While I was waiting for the doctor to arrive, Lois returned to the hospital and informed me that four-year-old Ardelle had fallen and was taken to a clinic for stitches. I remember thinking, *This reminds me of the story of Job.*

However, after only two weeks, Marilyn was dismissed from the hospital. Doctor Riche could only say that he did not understand her case. The spinal tests had indicated a severe attack, but although her speech and neck were definitely affected, the general condition of her body did not correspond with what had been anticipated. God had performed a miracle. Marilyn's speech continued to improve, and she was able to return to school for the second semester. Merle asked Dr. Riche, a professing agnostic, if he believed it was a miracle of God. Dropping his head, the doctor nodded slowly and answered, "Without doubt, without doubt."

The American military doctor who was stationed in Phnom Penh, having heard of Marilyn's illness, asked permission to see her. After a thorough examination and a detailed review of the case, he informed us that he was seventy percent sure that she had had an attack of bulbar polio. When Curwen Smith, the missionary who had anointed Merle and Marilyn, returned to Saigon by plane, he found himself seated next to the specialist with whom Dr. Riche had consulted.

"That is too bad about the pastor's daughter," said the doctor.

"Yes," replied Curwen. "I understand that she has spinal meningitis."

"No," said the doctor. "She has bulbar polio. The attending physician knew it from the beginning, but he felt that it was too awful to tell the pastor."

Both Marilyn and Merle recovered. A few weeks later, we received a letter from a friend in the Chicago area. "What happened to the Gravens?" she wrote. "I was awakened one night in November," (she gave the date) "and I felt a heavy burden for you. I had to pray." It was the exact time that Marilyn had lain critically ill in the hospital.

Meanwhile, the ministry at the International Exposition was very encouraging. It had been extended for an additional week, thus enabling Merle to recover sufficiently to attend the last several days.

Three thousand two hundred and sixty-four Cambodian gospels and books were sold, as well as several thousand Chinese and Vietnamese portions. Approximately 110,000 tracts had been distributed. People had come to the Expo from all sections of the land. For Cambodia, it had been an unprecedented opportunity for disseminating the Word.

Sensing that God had raised her up for a purpose, Marilyn later dedicated her life to God to prepare for missionary service. Tragedy had turned to triumph through the power of prayer.

Note

1. Louisa Graven, *Poems from the Heart* (Ft. Myers, FL, 2000).

9

Bronze Buddhas and Devil Strings

After ninety years as a French protectorate, Cambodia gained its independence on November 9, 1953. A new era had begun. The national flag now flew proudly from its flagpole. Cambodia had taken its place in the family of free nations and was emerging as a small but important little country.

The city of Phnom Penh was undergoing a great physical change as a building boom rapidly transformed the familiar skyline of Buddhist temples, ancient trees and nineteenth-century French-style villas. Streets were being widened and their low-lying areas filled in with the help of American economic aid. Countless bicycles and three-wheeled *cyclos,* as well as new American and European cars, filled the streets, creating traffic chaos. American technicians and military instructors were arriving at an accelerated pace. With spacious parks, flower-decked promenades along the river, tree-lined boulevards and new street lights, Phnom Penh was a lovely city, the "pearl of the Orient."

But food vendors, both stationary and on wheels, were still there, selling everything from rice to roasted bananas and sugar cane. There was still the "sidewalk dentist" with his crude, unsterilized instruments, pulling someone's tooth or placing a gold cap on another's. Coolies still moved with their burdens dangling from the ends of a pole laid across their shoulders. Women still squatted at open-air markets selling vegetables, tropical fruits, dried fish, spices and other wares. Ox carts groaned as families rode to town. Dilapidated buses filled to capacity rattled along, their roofs piled high with wood, grain and produce. Such was the contrast between the old and the new.

According to the Cambodian government's historical records, the origin of Phnom Penh goes back to 1434, when it was founded as the Khmer capital, but it did not become a permanent royal residence and capital of Cambodia until about 1867, during the reign of King Norodom. Situated along the Bassac and Tonle Sap Rivers at their junction with the Mekong, this picturesque city was originally built around the Royal Palace complex and Wat Preah Keo Morokot (Silver Pagoda), which was known for its silver-tiled floors. In the northern section of the city stands a hill. Atop this hill is a pagoda housing the ashes of the legendary Lady Penh whose discovery of a bronze Buddha inspired the settlement bearing her name.[1]

Around the middle of the twentieth century, the matter of improving the nation's educational facilities was given high priority. Between 1956 and 1958, approximately 300 new primary school classrooms and more than 50 secondary rooms, each accommodating 40 students, opened each year. The schools were coeducational, replacing the traditional, segregated system of schooling that had previously been in place. A university was also founded in Phnom Penh.

With the help of foreign aid, a new hospital was built, the first deep-sea port was created, a 133-mile highway from Phnom Penh to the seaport was constructed and the Pochentong Airport was improved.

Was a new day dawning for Cambodia? We certainly hoped so. But though the country was now relatively peaceful, the heart of man was not. Buddhism, the official state religion, had controlled the destiny and regulated the lives of millions of Cambodians down through the centuries. Multitudes remained lost in spite of all their efforts to gain merit. More than 2,700 imposing Buddhist temples, not counting innumerable shrines, spoke of satanic endeavor. Over 80,000 saffron-robed priests begged for food but could not provide the answer for man's greatest need.

As Merle sat in a temple one day conversing and sipping tea with some of the monks, he asked, "How long have you been in the priesthood?"

The responses ranged from two to twenty years.

"Do you know for sure that your sins are forgiven?" Merle queried.

"No, Mister," was the reply. "How can you know?"

What an open door for an explanation of the gospel message!

****

The first Protestant mission station in Cambodia was opened in Phnom Penh by Arthur and Esther Hammond, Christian and Missionary Alliance missionaries, in February 1923. Though the mission's early years had been fraught with opposition from both the French and the Cambodian governments and converts were few, the entire Bible had now been translated into the Cambodian language, and a hymnbook and other literature were available. The missionary endeavor had been interrupted by World War II and then by the fight for independence, but now missionaries were able to travel again with greater freedom and opportunities to spread the Word.

Over thirty years of Alliance ministry had passed, and there was still no church building for Cambodian Christians in Phnom Penh. The small, rented storefront building in which they had met in the pre-war days had been requisitioned by the military, and the Christians were forced to worship in a room under the mission guesthouse. Rent prices and the value of real estate were soaring. It appeared impossible to acquire land suitably located for the erection of an evangelistic center.

However, the Hammonds occupied a mission house that could be easily converted into a meeting place. It was strategically located on a busy thoroughfare of the city just a short distance from the main market. It could accommodate a lovely chapel and a bookstore where Cambodians could come at any time of the day to purchase books, read freely at tables and inquire concerning salvation. It would also be possible to hold evening services complete with a public-address system, show religious films and preach the Word. The house would even be able to accommodate students who were studying in the local high schools. Since some of the Christian young people from the provinces were forced to room with unbelievers or board in schools where they were not free to attend church regularly, this was definitely an advantage.

Arthur and Esther were willing to move if other living quarters could be provided for them. It was proposed and approved that a second story be added to the guesthouse, thus making possible two apartments for missionary residences.

When the construction work was completed and others could take charge, Merle and I asked permission to be relieved of some of our assignments, including the guesthome and business agency, in order to give our full time to spiritual ministry. Our request was granted. We would concentrate on the city of Phnom Penh and Kandal Province, which together made up one-fifth of Cambodia's population. Merle, of course, still remained as pastor of the International Church. We moved into a house built high on pillars in an area called Psa Suon, which means "garden market."

Scattered throughout Kandal Province were dozens of villages where the gospel had never been proclaimed. One Sunday afternoon several Christians accompanied us to witness in one of these villages. My heart was deeply moved when a man stepped forward with this question: "If the Christian religion is older than Buddhism, as you say it is, why is it that I am hearing about it today for the first time?"

Since children in Phnom Penh attended school on Saturdays and Thursdays were free days, we decided to take advantage of the opportunity to share the gospel with them. On Thursday mornings, we carried my folding organ, flannel board and easel down the numerous steps to the yard below. As soon as the first strains of music began, kids of all ages would come running from every direction, older ones carrying younger siblings on their hips. Occasionally, a mother or two would join us. The children were delighted to receive pretty, used Christmas cards as their reward for learning Scripture verses.

A few months later, given the shortage of staff and the proliferation of opportunities both near and far, we were asked to continue with the same assignments and to add Bible school ministry, a correspondence course and supervision of two additional provinces to our workload. Also, we would be moving once more back to the Bible school compound where Merle would assume directorship of the school, and we both would be teaching.

The Bible school was located at the southern edge of Phnom Penh near a small village called Ta Khmau, thus the name Ta Khmau Bible School. It was the only theological training school in all of Cambodia.

The compound was an oasis of tranquility from the hustle and bustle of the city. It was situated along the Bassac River, which flowed south for part of the year and reversed its flow during the other months. Near the river's edge, in the school's expansive front lawn, stood a large mango tree whose branches provided shade under which one could sit and rest. A porch ran the full width of the missionary residence both in front and in back. A bougainvillea vine with its vibrant red floral bracts graced the fence at the entrance to the grounds. A well-kept lawn with flowering bushes and shrubs, a fiery red canna bed and a frangipani tree with its fragrant waxy flowers of exquisite white all added to the serenity and beauty of the place.

The task of converting the missionary residence in Phnom Penh into a church was eventually finished. The Cambodian Christians were delighted to have their new place of worship. There was a chapel that could seat approximately 150, a bookstore and a reading room. Space was available for a studio where programs could be taped for broadcast from Manila. Under the house were three rooms filled with young high school students. There were more applications than we had space for, and the rooms were crowded.

Each Tuesday and Thursday night there were three classes going on simultaneously in the church. Young people from all over the city were studying English by reading Bible stories and the Gospels. Over 100 registered on opening day, with still others wanting to enroll. We simply lacked space and teachers.

Then the government made it possible for the mission to procure three lots in a fast-growing suburb. A building would be constructed to provide a youth center and another place of worship. The doors for an abundant future ministry were opening.

One exciting ministry was the youth conference, which was held annually on the Bible school grounds. It was 1959, and the seventh annual conference, scheduled to run for three weeks, was at hand. For months there had been much prayer and planning. We had spent hours searching for classroom supplies, handwork, sports equipment, rewards and other necessities. A fifth-year course of study had been added, making a total of twenty-three different subjects to be taught by eleven teachers. Bernard and Edythe Dunning had come to assist us full-time during the conference. Dormitory rooms and classrooms were readied to accommodate an anticipated attendance of eighty-five students ranging in age from fifteen through the early twenties.

On August 1, the youth began arriving by bus, train, boat and car. Excitedly, we went out to greet them. Our excitement turned to amazement as dormitory rooms began overflowing, and still they came, both Christians and unbelievers. Some had never attended a church service. One classroom became a dormitory room by night where a number of boys slept on the floor. Our office and front porch became two additional classrooms. Before registration was done, 109 had enrolled, 32 of whom were girls. (This was significant because at one time Cambodian parents hesitated to permit their daughters to go where there was a mixed group. But now the par-

ents trusted the missionary leadership and were allowing their daughters to come.) It was the highest
attendance for a Christian youth conference in
Cambodia to that date.

Each day began with an early morning prayer
meeting at 6:30 and closed with lights out at 10 each
night. In between were hours of study, handwork,
recreation and listening to the Word of God. From 9
to 9:30 p.m., missionaries and counselors met in various rooms for devotional reading and prayer with
the youth. It gave the young people an opportunity
to voice the burdens on their hearts. From the out-
set, an unusual hunger for God's Word was manifested, and the response to its appeal was almost
unbelievable. Discipline problems proved to be in-
significant.

Early in the first week, three non-Christian young
men requested to go home. Two of them had become ill. Admitting that they had "devil strings"—
strings worn on the body to appease evil spirits and
ensure good fortune—tied about their waists, they
said, "Christ has power over the devil. We feel His
presence, and we are afraid." They were not ready
to make a decision for Christ, so we reluctantly
watched them depart. However, we did have the joy
of seeing a devil string cut from the body of one of
the young women.

During the last ten days of the conference, Rev.
Dr. Ben Wati, the secretary of the Evangelical Fellowship of India, arrived to preach and counsel the
youth. Across the front of the chapel the conference
theme was written in large Cambodian letters: Jesus

Is Everything to Me. That theme became the testimony of many of the youth.

"I was an atheist when I arrived," testified one young man, "but after attending classes and studying the Word of God, I am persuaded that Jesus Christ is God. I gave my heart to Him this morning after chapel. I am fully aware of the persecution that I face upon my return to work."

"Mister," said another young man to Merle as he counted change given to him in return for a larger bill, "there is one *riel* too much in this change that you gave to me (approximately three cents US at that time). I gave my heart to Christ during this conference, and now I must be honest and tell you about it. Here it is."

On Sunday afternoons the young men went out witnessing in the surrounding villages. Even those who had just accepted Christ stated their desire to go and witness.

The closing days of the conference were especially memorable—a banquet, a program and the distribution of awards. The open-air auditorium was artistically decorated with palm branches and colorful streamers. Tables were arranged in long rows with name cards placed at each plate. Some of the young men served as waiters; others formed a clean-up crew to transform the same area into a meeting place for the evening program. Nearly every class participated in the program, displaying the knowledge they had acquired in their three weeks of study.

Before the conference ended, twenty had prayed for salvation and many more had come to the altar to repent of the sin in their lives. Several young men expressed their desire to give themselves to full-time Christian service upon completion of their studies in government schools.

When it was time to say farewell, many tears were shed and many months counted until everyone would meet again at the next conference. A frequently heard parting request was, "Please pray for me." The future of the Church of Jesus Christ in Cambodia looked brighter because of this moving of the Spirit among the youth.

Our home assignment was due in a few months. We were also expecting our third child. Ten days before my due date, I boarded an airplane alone for Bangkok, Thailand. Merle would take the two-day trip by train the following week when another missionary couple arrived to substitute for us in the school. We had written ahead for a missionary friend in Bangkok to meet me.

On board the plane I was pleased to find an American lady who attended the International Church in Phnom Penh. When we arrived at the Bangkok airport, she asked, "Do you have transportation into the city?"

"Yes," I replied. "I am expecting a missionary from our guesthome to meet me." But when I got to the terminal, I could find no one.

Shortly thereafter, the American lady found me. "The road into the city is closed because the king and queen of Thailand are arriving home from a trip to

Indonesia. I have an embassy car waiting that will be able to get through. Come with me, and we will take you to your destination."

I felt like a queen as the chauffeur-driven car sped past the police and guards to the door of the guest-home! Once again, I had experienced God's loving guidance and faithful provision.

The following week, we were blessed with a baby boy, whom we named Gordon Emerson. Arriving back in Phnom Penh, we finished teaching our classes in the school, attended the Cambodian National Conference and packed to leave for home assignment. We did not know it then, but years later we would remember this term as the most peaceful one we experienced in Cambodia.

Note

1. Ministry of Information, Phnom Penh, "Phnom Penh's Building Boom," *Cambodia Today*, March/April 1959, p. 10.

10

Lessons of Faith

While on home assignment, we were faced with a most difficult decision. The Division of International Ministries had a ruling that transportation to and from the field would not be provided for a teenager unless the teen had more than two years of high school remaining. Marilyn would be in her junior year when we returned to Cambodia.

Should we leave her in the States in a boarding school, or should we remain at home until she graduated? We discussed the matter with Marilyn, and she suggested that we return to Cambodia. "I only wish that I could go as a missionary now myself," she said. We gave Marilyn a choice of several Christian boarding schools. She chose Toccoa Falls Academy, which was in operation at that time.

Meanwhile, I was steadily losing weight and strength. I attributed it to a busy schedule, but then we noticed that one of my eyes was bulging. The ophthalmologist suspected a thyroid problem and recommended that I see an internist. The internist in turn referred me to a doctor doing thyroid research in Cleveland, Ohio. The diagnosis was confirmed. I had hyperthyroidism, which had resulted in Graves' disease.

"If you plan to return to Cambodia, you must either undergo major surgery or have radioactive iodine therapy," said the specialist. He described the advantages and disadvantages of each and left the choice to me. "But," he added, "if you were planning to remain in the States for a period of time, I would give medication instead and observe you for several months." It was as though I was at a fork in the road with three possible directions. Which one should I take? After prayer and consideration, I chose to submit to major surgery in order to return to Cambodia as soon as possible.

In the meantime, a letter arrived stating that the ruling regarding missionary teens had been changed. Transportation would be provided for Marilyn; she could return to Cambodia with us. But Marilyn had finalized her plans to enroll at the academy, and she chose to remain in the States. So, after helping her get settled in the dorm at Toccoa Falls, I returned home and entered the hospital for surgery.

God's perfect guidance was evident once more, for during surgery an inward goiter was discovered. "You made the right decision," said the doctor.

Two months later the internist informed me that he had to provide an opinion concerning whether or not I was able to return to the field. "How do you feel?" he asked. "If you want to return, I will give my approval. If you do not feel ready to go back, I will give a negative reply."

"I will go," I answered.

Before we left, Marilyn flew home for Thanksgiving. I can still remember the brave spirit of our sixteen-year-old girl when it was time for her to leave again. As she walked toward the plane she suddenly paused and said, "Mother, don't cry."

Early in December we boarded a plane for Cambodia. My right eye, still bulging quite noticeably, showed little, if any, improvement, and my strength was limited.

As we flew from Hong Kong to Cambodia, my heart was sorrowful. I had suddenly realized that I might never again see Marilyn while she was in her teen years. I gazed out the window of the plane. We were flying high above the clouds, and, looking down between them, I could see the jungle forests of Vietnam, where there was war and strife. But looking upward, there was nothing to obscure my vision—a cloudless blue sky, sunlight and serenity. I thought of a chorus that I had heard Marilyn sing:

> Back of the clouds, the sun is always shining,
> After the storms, your skies will all be blue;
> God has prepared a rosy-tinted lining,
> Back of the clouds, it's waiting to shine through.[1]

Somehow my burden seemed lighter. Eyes of faith must ever be focused upward. It is then that we see Him who is invisible.

Upon our return, Merle was reappointed to the directorship of the Bible school. We were both teaching, and of course there were other miscellaneous assignments and opportunities as well. Physically, it was not easy at first to maintain my teaching schedule. There were times when I returned from the classroom, knelt by my bed and prayed for strength to continue. But in due time my strength returned and my eye returned to normal.

Teaching in the Bible school was a great challenge and was very rewarding. It was also a tremendous responsibility to be involved in helping to train the future leaders of the Church. Standards were being raised and students were required to study for four years to obtain their diplomas. The school was attracting students with higher scholastic training, and single women were now accepted.

More music was added to the curriculum. A church in Georgia purchased a beautiful piano for the school, and two nice pump organs were donated. (There was no electricity at the school except that produced by a generator for a few hours each evening.) On weekends, students were busy in various types of Christian ministry, including a student choir and a male quartet, and several played musical instruments.

Culturally, it seemed like Cambodian youth were reaching out with hungry, inquiring hearts. There was a vacuum, an emptiness, a longing for something they did not have. With many new schools in the country, there were more opportunities for education, and with increased knowledge came the awareness that Buddhism could not meet their needs.

Youth meetings were begun in the school chapel on Saturday nights and led by a senior classman who was also president of the national Alliance youth organization. An interesting and varied program attracted many unsaved young people.

In the fall of 1962, the Spirit of God began to move in the area around the school. Young people by the score came to inquire about following Jesus. During a span of only nine days in December, our students prayed with a total of forty-six to receive Christ. Thirty-seven of them immediately enrolled in the Bible correspondence course on the Gospel of John.

There were early morning prayer meetings and testimonies full of victories, and the spirit of dedication among the students was very evident. One young couple had left their baby with her parents, sold their bicycle, wrapped the money in a piece of cloth and brought it to the school. "This is all that we have," they told Merle as they handed him the bundle. "May we both enroll and work to pay for our expenses?" God was preparing His leaders for the dark days ahead.

Kuch Kong and his family also lived on the Bible school compound. In addition to teaching, Kong (in general, Cambodian first names are family names, and second names correspond to American first names) was also the dean of men, and his wife, San, was the dean of women. Their conversion, which had taken place some years previously, was a remarkable testimony to the power of the printed word.

Kru Kong, meaning Teacher Kong, as he was called, had originally been a customs official. One day while busily searching the baggage of train passengers en route from Phnom Penh to Battambang, he came across several Cambodian gospel booklets. "What are these?" he asked.

The owner of the booklets did not answer because she herself did not really know. She had only accepted them from some Christian and stuck them in her bag. So Kong kept them and put them in his pocket. Later that day, he read and reread them. He liked what he read, and the next day he told some friends about the tracts.

"We know now that you are a Christian," they told him disparagingly.

"No," he retorted, "I'm a Buddhist, but this is good. I like it."

Some time later, Kong and his family moved to another city. In order to travel as lightly as possible, he threw the Christian literature into the waste basket. But while he was out of the house, San spied the booklets. *Those are too good to throw away,* she thought. So she packed them with their belongings.

While they were unpacking at their new house, Kong saw the booklets. "Where did these come from?" he asked.

"I found them in the trash, but they looked too nice to throw away, so I kept them," San answered.

Since the seed had been planted in his heart, Kong felt urged to locate someone who could explain to him more fully this new-birth religion. He found some Christians, and before long both he and San had prayed to receive Christ. Their lives had been dedicated to God and were now being used in special ministry at the Bible school.

* * * *

The water system at the school was unsatisfactory and inadequate. Our only source of water came from the river which flowed by the compound. This dirty, impure water was pumped into a vat. It was then settled with alum and pumped up into another vat. By sheer force of gravity, it flowed through pipes to the mission house. Drinking water had to be filtered and boiled for twenty minutes. A more sanitary system was needed.

United States Aid (USAID) had agreed to provide well-drilling rigs for the Cambodian government. The American technician who advised the government in the use of the rigs attended our International Church, and Merle approached him about the possibility of a well being drilled for the school. The technician suggested that Merle contact the director of USAID.

"Once the drilling equipment is put on the ship in the United States, we have no more jurisdiction over it," the director said. "Contact the Cambodian government."

So Merle went directly to the minister of health. "I will pay for the gasoline and pipe if you can provide the well-drilling equipment," Merle told him.

"I can tell you in advance that you will not find water," said the man. "The World Health Organization (WHO) has drilled in a number of places in your area. Every hole was dry."

"If you are willing to send your men," Merle responded, "I will trust my God for the water."

And so it was agreed. When the men and equipment arrived at the school some days later, they asked, "Where shall we drill?"

"Over there," said Merle, pointing to a spot where a vine was growing. They found water at 125 feet! It was warm, clean, soft and abundant, and what's more, it was sufficient to meet every need for the whole compound. Through the Lord's provision, we were also able to purchase an electric pressurized water pump.

Merle took a sample to the Institute Pasteur to have it tested. "Where did you get this water?" they asked. "We have never seen any water so pure in all of Cambodia." The WHO sent representatives down to the school to inquire how we had found the water. From our viewpoint it was God's miracle well, a testimony again of His loving care and provision.

But amidst all of the blessings we were enjoying around the school, the nation's political scene was beginning to change. Dark clouds were appearing on the horizon.

Note

1. Carolyn R. Freeman, "Back of the Clouds," copyright 1931, renewal 1959, Word Music, LLC. Used by permission.

11

The Shadows Lengthen

Communism was slowly but surely extending its tentacles into every part of Cambodian society. It had infiltrated the Normal School for training teachers. It had reached into the public schools. It had gained entrance into the Bureau of Information, thereby controlling the propaganda. Soon an air of uncertainty was hanging over that graceful land.

In the midst of the darkening political clouds, one of our veteran missionaries, David Ellison, had a heart attack and went to be with the Lord. His memorial service, held on the Bible school grounds, was moving and victorious. A missionary male quartet sang "He the Pearly Gates Will Open," and certainly David had had an abundant entrance. He had faithfully sown the seed, the Word of God, through many difficult days. Now God had chosen to give him the privilege of remaining in Cambodian soil. Would that seed someday produce a harvest in Cambodia? We believed it would.

In November 1963, the head of state, Prince Sihanouk, announced that no more American aid would be accepted and that all USAID personnel must leave Cambodia immediately. From that time on, anti-American propaganda filled the airwaves. Then the Cambodian ambassador was recalled from Washington, DC. We wondered, *Would diplomatic relations be broken and all Americans have to leave on very short notice?* We didn't know, but we packed some bags, just in case; then we continued our work as usual.

In the midst of all this political and personal uncertainty, our son Gordon became ill with a severe sore throat and broke out with the three-day measles. He was very sick, and we were concerned. Then the Lord gave Merle a promise from First Chronicles 28:20:

> Be strong and courageous, and do the work. Do not be afraid or discouraged, for the LORD God, my God, is with you. He will not fail you or forsake you until all the work for the service of the temple of the LORD is finished.

Gordon recovered, and we had a new peace in our hearts that God—not the government—was truly in charge and that we were safe in His care as long as He wanted us there.

Then one day the chilling air of shock and sobriety blew hard over the student body. We received news that Vorn, who had been a student and a friend to many, had died. Vorn's contagious smile had revealed only part of his pleasing personality; his deft hands were always helpful and ready to assist with anything there was to be done.

Vorn had not returned to school the second semester, sensing the need to help his parents harvest

an abundant rice crop. They had just obtained a tractor, which was a rarity for farmers in those days. So
Vorn had requested permission to register a few days
late; however, one month had already passed since
the start of school.

Finally one day during the chapel period, Vorn entered the room and sat down in the front row. One
glance at him revealed a pale, gaunt and fevered
face, a picture of death itself. We immediately took
Vorn to the hospital, where he was diagnosed with
typhoid fever.

Twelve days later, on February 15, 1964, as Merle
and a student gospel team were engaged in a weekend ministry in Battambang, a telegram arrived stating, "Vorn died at 6 a.m. today." Would it have been
different if Vorn had returned to school? No one
could answer that question. But one thing we did
know: Vorn's untimely death prodded the students
into a closer walk with God and to a greater determi-
nation to do His will.

Our suitcases had been packed for several weeks.
With the political situation seemingly under control,
I decided that it was time to unpack them. However,
a few weeks later in March a big anti-American demonstration took place. Both the American and the
British embassies were attacked, and the American
library was completely destroyed. Then came an incident on the Cambodian-Vietnamese border in-
volving the death of seventeen Cambodians. Ten-
sions mounted again. Cambodians threatened to

hold another anti-American demonstration. American government wives and children were evacuated, and the American Consul urged the missionaries to do likewise.

The Bible school was scheduled to close on April 10, which was in approximately three more weeks. We were preparing and practicing for the commencement program at which time two young men would be receiving their diplomas. Both So Nan and Tuy Sreng had been former Buddhist monks. So Nan had worn the saffron-colored robe for six years, and Tuy Sreng for three years, but they had been transformed by the power of God to become priests unto Himself. Their lives had unquestionably proven their love and loyalty to Jesus Christ. The story of So Nan's conversion revealed the importance and reward of personal witnessing:

Along a busy, crowded street in Phnom Penh city walked a small, middle-aged Cambodian woman. She was neither educated nor learned; she could neither read nor write in her native tongue. She was dressed very simply, for she had little of this world's goods. Yet she was rich, because she had heard the gospel message and had put her faith in Christ. Each day she made her way to a nearby market called the Garden Market to do a bit of selling so that she and her husband might have a few more *riels*.

Down this same street, from the opposite direction, walked another woman. Her face betrayed the many years she had spent in darkness and under the influence of evil spirits. She had spent a fortune trying to free herself from the power of these spirits, but to no avail. Fear and hopelessness were written all over her face. Then, in God's providence, she met the Christian lady at Garden Market, who witnessed to her and invited her to visit the Cambodian church to hear more of the gospel.

Later, the woman indicated that she would like to receive Christ, but the spirits would not let her believe. In fact, it seemed that the more she wanted to believe, the more the demons fastened their grip on her. Then one day the missionaries prayed and commanded the demons to depart from the woman's life and her home in the name of the Lord Jesus Christ. She destroyed her charms, her fetishes, her prayer books written to the devil and the tiger's tooth she carried in her mouth. We called her the Mary Magdalene of Cambodia. Saved from devastating bondage, she was now faithfully attending church and witnessing to the power of Christ.

Some time later, another pair of brown feet walked down another busy street. They belonged to a Buddhist monk who, with his rice bowl suspended from his shoulder and hidden from view, went out each morning to collect food for the day. The peace for which he was searching had eluded him, but one day, after leaving the priesthood, he heard the story of God's power from the lips of the "delivered one" ("Mary Magdalene"), who in turn invited him to go to church with her. There So Nan too found Christ and went on to Bible school, where he would receive his diploma after four years of study.

So Nan had paid much of his tuition by selling gospel books, so it was natural that he would become a colporteur for the British and Foreign Bible Society. His feet were now walking for the Master. "How beautiful are the feet of those who bring good news!" (Romans 10:15).

Tuy Sreng's mother had accepted Christ before Sreng did. To show his distaste for the gospel, Sreng would sometimes hide his mother's food while she was asking God's blessing upon it. Then, at the age of twenty-four, Sreng was genuinely born again. Once a Buddhist monk, he would upon graduation become an evangelical pastor.

The last social event of the school year was scheduled to be held in our home on Friday evening, March 27. An American lady had given me a large ham and a few boxes of cake mix. The students were looking forward to the event.

Despite ongoing pressure from the embassy for at least the women and children to leave, I told Merle, "I cannot evacuate now. I want to finish out the school year. I'll wait until you go or at least until classes are finished."

On Thursday, March 26, another anti-American demonstration seemed imminent. I finally decided to leave Cambodia the following Monday with the last group of women. That same evening the Bible school committee met to discuss whether or not it seemed feasible to continue the school in light of the present circumstances. With all of the women leaving, the teaching staff would be severely reduced; there were also single girls at the school for whom we were responsible. Merle returned home that night and reported, "The committee has voted to close the school tomorrow."

"Tomorrow!" I exclaimed. "What about the commencement exercises? The graduates will be very disappointed. And what about the social for tomorrow night—and that big ham?"

After some discussion, we decided to hold both the commencement program and the social the following night. When morning dawned, we began to organize our work. Merle was called into Phnom Penh for an emergency meeting of the evacuation committee. Meanwhile, I spent the day making last-minute preparations. Thankfully, we managed to get everything done on time, and the students thoroughly enjoyed the ham sandwiches and cupcakes.

On Monday morning, four-year-old Gordon and I walked out of our home, said good-bye to Merle and the Christians on the school compound and flew to Dalat School in Vietnam to join Ardelle. Now only six missionary men remained in Cambodia: Harry Taylor, Bliss Steiner, Joe Doty, Ed Thompson, Paul Ellison and Merle.

Safely in Dalat, Gordon and I moved into the lower level of a cottage. But we were not alone. At night, I could hear a rat scampering through the kitchen across from our bedroom as he busied himself at destruction—until I finally caught him. Gordon became ill with a sore throat and a fever, and I learned that my husband's life was being threatened back in Cambodia. Although the climate was pleasant and the spring nights cool, I was feeling a bit discouraged.

One morning, I knelt on the cold cement floor by the sofa and asked the Lord to give me a message for that day. I opened my Bible to Hebrews 12 and began to read. When I reached verse two, the Holy Spirit began to speak to my heart:

> Let us fix our eyes on Jesus, the author and perfecter of our faith, who for the joy set before him endured the cross, scorning its shame, and sat down at the right hand of the throne of God. Consider him who endured such opposition from sinful men, so that you will not grow weary and lose heart. In your struggle against sin, you have not yet resisted to the point of shedding your blood. (12:2-4)

This was the message I needed. It would provide strength for endurance in the days ahead.

Back in Cambodia, the National Church Conference was being held on the Bible school grounds. One evening some Christians came excitedly to Merle, saying, "Mister, Mister, there are some men standing outside the gate who are threatening to come in, burn the buildings and kill you."

"Don't worry," said Merle. "The Lord will take care of us."

And He did. God intervened once again, and the threats did not materialize.

After approximately one month, the other women and I were able to return to Cambodia, but dark forebodings continued to hover over the land. Missionary visas were being issued for shorter periods of time and were eventually refused renewal.

We were also conscious that our activities were always under surveillance; it seemed like a hundred eyes were constantly peering at us. One day, a stranger came to the school office. "I heard that you spoke at a youth gathering recently," he said, confronting Merle. "What did you speak about?" Merle pulled out his sermon and began to preach it to the man. The man soon left.

In one town, a spy attended the chapel every Sunday to see who had dared to come. Names were recorded, and occasionally the man followed a new convert home. The Bible school students were also being watched, especially when they visited certain areas to witness, distribute tracts and sell Christian literature.

It was December 1, 1964. Preparations were being made for a Christmas program and a school banquet to climax the first semester. Merle and I received the disturbing news that our resident visa, which was to expire December 12, would not be renewed. That was only eleven days away and school was not scheduled to end until December 18! How would it be possible, among numerous other duties, to train a new director for the school who, because of the situation, would now be a national?

San Hay Seng, the son of an idol-maker known in Cambodia as Lim Chheong, was chosen to assume the directorship. He had once declined the opportunity to study and obtain a government position in the field of meteorology, and the decision had incurred the wrath of his father. But like Moses, San Hay Seng "regarded disgrace for the sake of Christ as of greater value than the treasures of Egypt, because he was looking ahead to his reward" (Hebrews 11:26).

San Hay Seng was a graduate of Ta Khmau Bible School, had studied abroad for one year at Ebenezer Bible College in the Philippines and was now back serving as a teacher at his alma mater. He had married a lovely young woman, Hana, who was one of the Bible school students. They would move into the home that we were about to vacate.

Should I stop my work and pack? I thought of it all: Christmas program rehearsals, preparations for the banquet, classes to finish teaching, second semester music material to get in order for the next teacher, the annual report for the correspondence course, and so the list went. I chose to continue with my busy schedule, leaving the packing for any spare moments that I could find. Thankfully, the Cambodian government agreed to give us two additional weeks in which to leave the country.

One night I walked out on the front porch of our home. A full moon was shining down on the Bassac River, reflecting its face in the dark water which flowed so peacefully toward the South China Sea. A big mango tree stood gracefully silhouetted in the moonlight. The grass covered the lawn as a verdant carpet, for the rainy season had only recently ended.

To my left was a tall bougainvillea plant with its large clusters of red flowers; to my right, a dormitory filled with students whom God had called and sent to be trained for His service. The sweet scent of a gardenia bush filled the night air. It was a picture of beauty and serenity. *Why,* I wondered, *are we packing to leave this beautiful place?* It didn't seem possible that the doors were actually closing on us.

Little piles here, little piles there. Some destined to be put into suitcases, some to be packed in barrels in case we could sometime return, another pile to give to the students. I was attempting to pack, but time was running out.

As I said farewell to the young women, one of them said, "It is not going to be the same here anymore when you go."

"Stay true to God no matter what it costs," I urged them. "Though persecutions and trials face you, what you must endure is only for a moment compared to eternity. Never give up your faith in God."

"We want to stay true and serve God," came the reply. "Pray for us."

On Monday, December 21, we walked once again out of our Cambodian home. The curtains were still hanging in the windows; a favorite picture still hung on the wall. The following day, we flew to Bangkok, Thailand. Some of the students and staff came to the airport to see us off and to present us with souvenirs. Realizing the sacrifice they had made to purchase them, we knew the gifts were very precious.

But the most moving of all were words spoken by a senior student to Merle that last morning. He said, "There are two things for which I am thankful: one, that Christ has saved me and I am a Christian. The second is that I have been privileged to study with you. You have been an example to us." That was why we were there—to honor God and bring glory to Him through both our words and our deeds.

We waited in Bangkok for a few days, hoping that the Cambodian government would change its policy. When that did not occur, we flew on to the States so that Ardelle could enter the second semester of school, and we began a year of home assignment.

After our home assignment was up, we chose not to transfer to another mission field. We wanted to be free to return to Cambodia if and when it reopened. Merle accepted a call to pastor the Havelock church (now Rosemont) in Lincoln, Nebraska, the same church he had once served as youth pastor. But I felt in my heart that someday we would return to Cambodia.

Merle as a student at the Missionary Training Institute (now Nyack College). God's call dramatically changed the course of his life.

This picture was taken when I was twenty-one years old. I gave up a teaching career, or so I thought, to follow God's leading. He gave teaching back to me in Cambodia.

Marilyn was just three years old when we went to Cambodia.

Our first home in Battambang was formerly a Bible school dormitory. When I first saw it, I was reminded of a barn, and I soon found that its crudely constructed interior was home to many creatures, including cockroaches and geckos.

Harold and Marguerite Sechrist, with little Ruth Ann, were senior missionaries on the station. We shared many interesting experiences with them.

The mission residence in Battambang. It was under this home that the Issarak rebels hid in order to ambush the French police commissioner.

We bounced over many rough and dangerous roads in this little Renault, but it served us well.

Many Cambodian homes are built on posts and entered by way of ladder-like steps. Livestock make their home under the house.

The Alliance church in Battambang was the only Protestant church building in the country at that time.

This two-wheeled vehicle, which is pulled by a bicycle, is called a *remorque*. *Remorques* are one of the major modes of transportation in Cambodian towns and villages.

The ornate architecture of this temple is typical of the more than 2,700 Buddhist temples that dotted the Cambodian landscape.

Ed Roffe and Merle prepare for an airdrop of literature to villages that were impossible to reach by land because of rebel activity.

Yon picked up one of these "tracts from the sky" and found the Lord as his Savior.

In 1955 we returned to Cambodia with Ardelle Joanne (left), who was born in 1951, and Marilyn, who was then ten years old.

The Bible school compound was in a beautiful location along the Bassac River near a village called Ta Khmau.

Tuy Sreng (left) and So Nan proudly display their graduation diplomas. Both had once served as Buddhist monks.

Every Bible school student was involved in a practical ministry assignment. Teams witnessed in outlying villages, and the choir and musical groups participated in church services, evangelistic outreach, school programs, etc.

Gordon Emerson joined our family in 1960. Shortly after his birth we packed to leave for home assignment.

This Cambodian woman agreed to have her picture taken as she was returning home from market.

Gordon loved to play with our dog, Frisky, on the expansive Bible school lawn.

The government loaned Merle a helicopter, complete with a pilot, a gunner and a full complement of ammunition, for a one-day evangelistic visit to the town of Takeo.

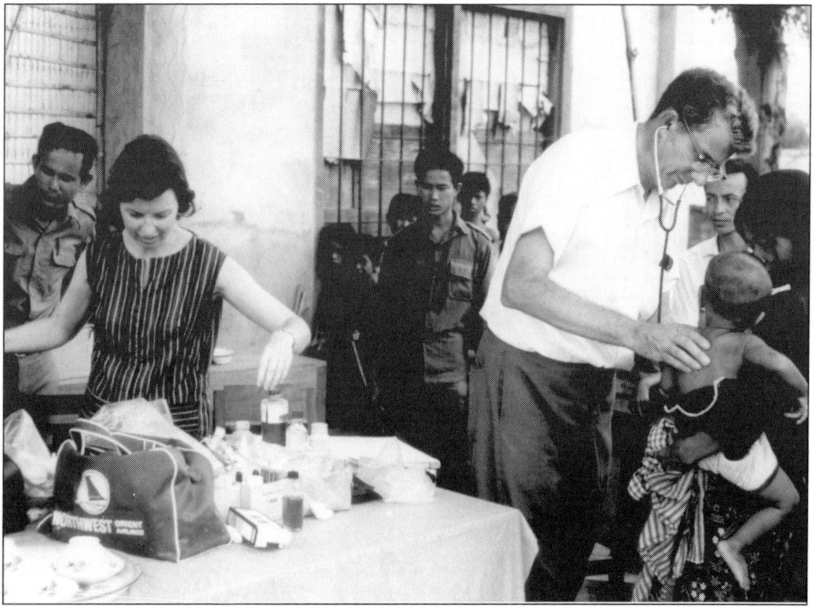

Dr. Dean Kroh and nurse Mary Lou Rorabaugh accompanied Merle to minister to the physical needs of the people.

A seemingly endless line of Buddhist monks, part of the more than
80,000 in the country, march on one of the main streets in Phnom Penh.
The monks lived on temple grounds and begged for their food on the streets.
The monks were available for merit-making ceremonies at many events.

A baptismal service in the Bassac River brought tears to my eyes. Fourteen of those baptized
were Mnong tribesmen who had lived in hidden villages in the mountains of northeastern
Cambodia. Their lives had been filled with superstition, fear and witchcraft.

In 1972, two citywide crusades were held in Phnom Penh with Dr. Stanley Mooneyham (center) as the evangelist. In the April crusade, thousands of people flooded the auditorium, so many that some had to be turned away on the first day. Over 3,200 people accepted Christ as a result of the two crusades. Son Sonne (left) served as translator. Merle is shown on the right.

The Palermo Brothers, musicians for the crusade, appeared on the local television station.

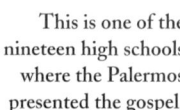

This is one of the nineteen high schools where the Palermos presented the gospel.

Sin Sum, a school teacher, found the Lord during the first crusade and became a firebrand for God. Along with his wife, Kao, Sin Sum worked in the refugee camps, delivering hope to the thousands who had fled from the Pol Pot forces.

As the Pol Pot forces overran villages and left death and destruction behind them, those who were fortunate enough to survive sought refuge in "God's Place," a camp set up by Sin Sum and Kao. There people were fed and exposed to the Word of God.

Merle taught conversational English to a class of Buddhist monks at the Buddhist university. He was allowed to use the Bible in some of his discussions, and the monks eagerly accepted Gideon New Testaments at the end of the year.

A Japanese war reparation bridge across the Tonle Sap River in Phnom Penh. It was completely destroyed by sappers one nights.

Minh Thien Voan, who had a master's degree from the University of Georgia, declined evacuation because of his deep burden for his parents and siblings. He became one of the first Christian martyrs.

During the war, Major Taing Chhirc returned prematurely from his doctoral studies in Edinburgh, Scotland, to witness for Christ to his people. He too became one of the martyrs.

Refugees in Sa Kaeo Camp (above), who lived in primitive, makeshift shelters (left) waited patiently each morning for their daily rations.

We often taught scriptural truths to small groups who gathered in one of these shelters. The man in the foreground, Lann Rin, was our first convert in the camp. He eventually came to the U.S. where he serves as a pastor.

When the Vietnamese army moved in, thousands of Cambodians fled to refugee camps in Thailand. The second time Merle visited Sa Kaeo Camp he had the privilege of preaching to a large and growing congregation of new believers.

A Cambodian congregation in Arlington, Virginia, one of nearly forty other Cambodian Alliance congregations who meet weekly. There are presently 200,000 Cambodians living in the United States.

Rev. Hiepson Kaysarn, pastor of the congregation in Arlington, and his wife, Sean.

Our children, L to R: Gordon, Ardelle and Marilyn.

Merle and Louisa Graven,
1994. We retired in 1990 after
forty-eight years of ministry
with The Christian and
Missionary Alliance.

12

A Miracle of Modern Missions

It had been nearly five years since we had left Cambodia when the telephone rang in October of 1969. A voice from the Division of International Ministries said, "We think that we can get some missionaries back into Cambodia. The national church has requested your return. We know that you have just dedicated a new church building, but would you pray about it?"

With mixed emotions, Merle promised to seek the Lord's guidance and give a reply. We were faced with a major decision. Our congregation had just relocated into a new developing area called Rosemont, and a beautiful new church complex had been dedicated only two months prior. We were happy to be there and were excited by all the opportunities that lay ahead. War was still going full-scale in Vietnam, and the situation in Cambodia was very unstable. The door could close at any time. Furthermore, Ardelle was a senior in high school. Returning to Cambodia would involve another heartrending farewell as we left behind our teenage daughter, knowing we may not see her again for four years.

Several weeks elapsed. Then Merle said, "I am going into the bedroom behind a closed door and will not come out until I have an answer from the Lord." While praying and reading from the book of Jeremiah, the Lord spoke to him:

> This is what the LORD says: "Whoever stays in this city will die . . . but whoever goes . . . will live. He will escape with his life; he will live." (38:2)

"I'm ready to die," replied Merle, "but I would like to live until my young son is grown."

"Then go," spoke the Lord to his heart.

Ardelle, of course, was disappointed that our return to Cambodia came too late for her to accompany us. Shortly after her high school graduation, we began to make preparations to leave the Rosemont pastorate.

In the meantime, the Khmer parliament had voted unanimously to oust Prince Sihanouk as chief of state. Now the war was spilling over from Vietnam into Cambodia, and the situation was becoming more uncertain by the day. "If you don't think of yourself, at least think of your wife and children," voiced one of the church members. But God had spoken. There was no turning back.

Ardelle chose to enroll in Nyack College. In September we drove her to the school and said a difficult good-bye. Gordon would be attending fifth grade at the Dalat School, which had been moved to Malaysia. Since classes had begun early in August, I endeavored to homeschool him while packing and traveling. It would be Gordon's first time away at boarding school.

Marilyn had married Fred Smith following their graduation from Toccoa Falls College in 1967, and after having served in a pastorate in Stillwater, Oklahoma, they had been appointed as missionaries to Peru, South America. Our family would be scattered over four countries and three continents.

War spread quickly across Cambodia. The only way in and out of Phnom Penh was by air. The Khmer Rouge guerrillas had choked off all highways leading to South Vietnam, Thailand and Laos. Our baggage would have to be shipped to Singapore and wait there for a boat going up the Mekong River to Phnom Penh. Since convoys on the river were subject to attack, we had no idea if or when our luggage might arrive.

Who were these soldiers called the Khmer Rouge? (The name means "red Cambodians.") They were a disparate combination of leftists and nationalists, an ill-defined marriage of convenience among Cambodian dissidents. Among them were supporters of the deposed Prince Sihanouk and Cambodian young people opposed to the new regime and to the military intervention of the United States and South Vietnam in their country. There were also some who had trained in North Vietnam. In addition, the Khmer Rouge forced young teens from occupied territory to join them in the jungles where they were indoctrinated and taught to become ruthless soldiers.

By the time we arrived, a significant portion of the Cambodian countryside was in communist hands.

Tens of thousands were fleeing the rubble that once had been quiet little villages, most of them hoping to find safety in the capital city of Phnom Penh.

On hand to greet us at the airport were church leaders and three missionary couples: Jean and Myrtle Fune, who had spent the past four years in Cambodia under the French Alliance; Jean-Jacques and Maria Piaget, a young couple in language study, also under the French Alliance; and Gene and Carol Hall, who had recently returned to Cambodia.

The national church committee had scheduled a meeting to be held the day after our arrival. Missionaries, church leaders and local elders were present. The Cambodian Christians recounted the experiences they had had during the years of our absence, but looked upon those years as a time when God was teaching His Church in Cambodia the meaning of responsibility and duty. The urgency of the hour was emphasized, and the Cambodians requested that a committee made up of both nationals and missionaries be formed to oversee the work of the Lord in Cambodia.

A dinner had also been arranged at a Chinese restaurant with twenty-five or more present. Among the guests was the undersecretary of the Ministry of Cults. He sat to Merle's right and was exceedingly genial and readily inquired of the gospel. He had come at the invitation of the national church leaders, who obviously desired to promote a good relationship between the new government and the Church.

The spirit of the churches was tremendous. We had never seen a time of greater expectancy among them; they were fast becoming witnessing churches. Persecution and suffering had only driven their roots deeper in the grace of God and firmly proven their faith. We were soon to see a moving of the Holy Spirit that would be termed "The Miracle of Modern Missions."

For the next two years, there would be only three missionary couples on the field at a given time. Our denominational headquarters appointed Merle as board representative with administrative oversight of the work. We moved into the mission guesthouse, and once again that ministry would be one of my responsibilities. There was no office help, so I also became the mission bookkeeper. In addition, Merle and I both taught in the Bible school.

In due time, our baggage arrived by boat convoy up the Mekong River. A bullet had penetrated one of the barrels, doing only minor damage.

That Christmas, a church on Monivong Boulevard was to be opened again for the first time in over five years. The believers diligently labored to make it attractive. It was freshly calcimined inside and out, a lovely platform was built, a new railing was erected around the altar, and the electric organ, which had been inactive for so long, was again in place. One of the Christians, an excellent artist, painted a large Christmas scene to grace the chapel. A youth choir and a children's choir would participate in the service. A few government officials were invited, and ushers proudly conducted them and others to the padded chairs that had been rented for the occasion. On December 24 at 4 p.m., the church was filled to capacity, with some standing in the foyer and many others peering in from the outside.

The following morning, another program was presented in the Tuol Ta Poung church, where Christians had been meeting for the past several years. Again, an overflow crowd was present. This congregation decided to take a step of faith. It would mother two churches, the one on Monivong Boulevard and another in a former Vietnamese church. Leaders were chosen, and Christian families were urged to attend the church nearest to them. As a result, attendance on the first Sunday that all three churches were open increased by nearly thirty percent, and the combined offerings were more than double. As it would turn out, this was the beginning of a tremendous multiplication of churches that would take place. The mother church was called "Bethlehem." The church on Monivong Boulevard was identified as "Bethany."

Other things were changing as well. Cambodia was now referred to as the Khmer Republic. The street on which we lived was renamed October 9 Boulevard in commemoration of the day that the country was declared a republic. Monivong Boulevard had become Independence Boulevard. These new names were symbolic of what was transpiring. The old was passing away in favor of the new. Old traditions and superstitions were giving way under the strain of war, increased education and the power of the gospel of Christ.

Merle and I were designated to work with the Bethany church. Three qualified laymen, all university graduates, would lead the congregation.

The first elder, Minh Thien Voan, had earned a scholarship to the University of Georgia. Not long after his arrival there, he had become acquainted with a staff worker from Campus Crusade. Later, when invited to a Bible study, Voan reluctantly went, but made it clear that he had no intention of becoming a Christian—he was a conservative Buddhist. However, during one of the Bible studies, he was deeply impressed with the words of John 3:16. After reading the Bible one night in his room, he made a decision. "Lord," he prayed, "you know how difficult it will be when I return home, but I want you to be my Savior." That was the beginning of Voan's relationship with God; it was a genuine conversion.

After receiving a master's degree in 1968, Voan returned home. He immediately faced several obstacles. There was the disapproval of parents who had expected him, their eldest son, to continue the family ancestral worship. And, since he had renounced Buddhism, he would not find employment in the Ministry of Education. Also, Voan did not know any Cambodian Christians, so he wondered where he would find a wife.

Voan sought out the only Protestant church in the city, the Khmer Evangelical Church, and attached himself to it. His testimony was a great encouragement to the Christians there and opened up a new dimension of witness. Voan was able to attract university students and influential government leaders to the church. At the National Church Conference in 1970, he was elected as an advisor and leader of the youth ministry.

God also provided Voan with a high-ranking position with Shell Oil Company. But as Voan grew in the Lord, his heart longed to give his full time to Christian service. In 1973, he gave up his lucrative position and became World Vision's deputy director in the Khmer Republic.

The Lord also provided Voan with a lovely wife from a Christian family. He chose to have the official announcement of the engagement take place following a Sunday morning service. After a sermonette by one of the church leaders, Voan, his fiancée and their parents walked to the front of the church, where Voan's mother placed a beautiful large ring on the young lady's finger. God had provided Voan with a Christian partner.

A second elder at Bethany Church was Major Taing Chhirc (CHHEE-uk). He was a third-generation Christian, his grandmother having been one of the earlier converts. Major Chhirc was a brilliant young man whose only desire had been to have an education, wealth and fame. He was a university graduate with the equivalent of a master's degree.

One day, as he read Galatians 2:20, he was impressed with these words: "I have been crucified with Christ." He sought the Lord and considered these words for two days and two nights. Then he made a decision and wrote in his diary, "I am dead. Chhirc is dead—dead to the world and all desires of the flesh." All of his previous ambitions became as toys, he testified. They were worthless things that could be thrown away. He was sold out to Christ.

Chhirc became a major in the army at a young age and was given a number of very responsible tasks. Great Britain offered him a scholarship to pursue his studies for a Ph.D. in Edinburgh, Scotland, but Chhirc preferred witnessing for the Lord, working with the youth, helping with the Gideons and assisting in relief work. He prolonged accepting the scholarship until he was informed that it was his last chance. Reluctantly he went to Scotland in February 1972 and was later joined by his wife, Bophana.

Hearing of God's outpoured blessing upon the Cambodian Church and greatly burdened for his people, Chhirc returned home in October 1973. He was restored to his former position as personal secretary to his superior, who was now the minister of defense, and given a temporary leave from his studies.

The third elder was Tan Van Jean, a captain in the Cambodian army reserves and brother-in-law of Major Chhirc. He was employed at the local government bank.

Since these three men were responsible for Bethany Church, they asked to meet with Merle for instruction in church organization, pastoral leadership and sermon preparation. One year later, Bethany Church had outgrown its mother church.

We were living in a country where war not only seemed inevitable but was now beginning. Even though I knew the war had begun, I was at first mys-

tified to notice the curtains in the guesthome sway-
ing without any apparent reason. Also, our bed
would occasionally shake. I soon learned that these
things were caused by the reverberation from bombs
exploding in the distance. Before long, the bombs
were dropping nearer and could be clearly heard.

Approximately three months after our arrival, we
were awakened one night by the sound of loud explosions. Brilliant flashes of fire lit up the western
sky; the airport was under attack. There had been ru-
mors that the Khmer Rouge forces were planning to
capture the airport and march into the city. Knowing
that there were no other means of escape, but re-
membering the promise God had given him, Merle
said, "I'm going back to bed. If the Lord neither
slumbers nor sleeps, I do not need to stay awake."

A high percentage of the Cambodian air force
planes were destroyed that night. Many pilots who
were required to sleep there for emergency purposes
were killed. However, the Khmer Rouge were re-
strained by the hand of the invisible God. There was
a harvest of souls yet to be reaped.

13

Just in Time

"**Y**ou're just in time." These words greeted me as I entered the hospital ward where I had gone to visit a young lady who had just graduated from Ta Khmau Bible School. Keim Ny had been hospitalized for an infection, and I found her staying in a ten-bed ward. Five beds were lined on each side of the room, and each bed was occupied. The patients ranged from children to older women. There was no privacy, no curtains to pull between the beds. There were always others present since it was customary for relatives to stay with the patients.

Keim Ny had almost left Bible school once because she wondered why she was there—perhaps it was only because that was what her parents had wanted her to do. Then, one day God had showed Keim Ny that she could be a soul winner for Him, and she began to share her faith with others.

When Keim Ny had entered the hospital, she had not been ill enough to be confined to bed, and she was anxious to share her faith. But how could she begin? Then she came up with an idea: In front of everyone, she would open her Bible and read. Then she would bow her head and pray. Perhaps someone would notice and ask, "What are you doing?" or "What are you reading?" Keim Ny's idea worked, and soon she was witnessing to those in the ward. She gathered the children around her bed, taught them choruses and told them Bible stories. Even doctors and interns heard her testimony.

One day a hospital employee asked, "Why are you here? To preach?"

"That's it," Keim Ny replied with a smile.

A young lady, the wife of a soldier, was in bed number one. The Khmer Rouge and Viet Cong had attacked her town, and one of her legs had been badly injured in the battle. It was in a cast and the woman was in great pain. Keim Ny prayed for her and then said with confidence, "God can help you." That night, the doctor came unexpectedly into the room and adjusted the cast, making it more comfortable. This seemed to be a direct answer to Keim Ny's prayer.

When I walked into the hospital ward that day, Keim Ny was sitting by the woman's bedside. "You're just in time to help me pray with this young lady to accept Christ," she exclaimed.

I would never forget those words. Merle and I had been given the privilege of going back "just in time" to witness a marvelous moving of the Holy Spirit in a land that had been spiritually barren for so long.

Mrs. Hay (Hi) was the wife of Cambodia's top-rated lettering artist. She had a heart condition and had spent a lot of money on medicines and attempts to appease the spirits. One night she had a dream that someone would come who could tell her how to get well, and the very next day a Christian worker went to her house on a business errand. While there, the worker witnessed to Mrs. Hay and her family about the Lord Jesus. Their hearts were touched, and four members of the family prayed for salvation—the father, the mother and two older children. They threw away their valuable Buddhist pictures and relics.

Not long afterward, Lean, Mrs. Hay's son, came excitedly to our house one Monday morning. "The Lord has blessed us so," he said. "He has given us a car. Yesterday I put a thousand *riels* in the church offering. Today, the Lord has given us more work than we can do."

Each Sunday the Hay family rode to church in their car. Since the father could not drive, he designated four persons who would have permission to drive. On Sunday afternoons, they filled the car with gospel literature and Christian laymen and went out to witness. On the car was inscribed the phrase, "This is Jesus' car." Mrs. Hay testified freely that she was trusting God to heal her of her heart condition, and she didn't spare herself in caring for her family and actively attending church services.

One morning some time later, as we were eating breakfast, we saw two persons coming up the front steps. One of them was a woman who was unkempt and looked to be demon-possessed. A second glance told us that it was Mrs. Hay accompanied by Lean. She had become very ill and had entered a Chinese hospital. Then, deciding that she wanted to trust Jesus to heal her, she had left. But now her mind appeared affected. All night she had bothered her family with incessant talking, laughing and cursing. Her long hair was uncombed, her head moved perpetually and there was a wild look in her eyes. She repeated everything Merle said, laughed and frequently mentioned Jesus' name.

Sensing that it was a demonic situation, Merle asked Mrs. Hay, "Do you still possess some idols or pictures of Buddha in your home?"

"Yes," she answered.

"Then you must go home and destroy them all," Merle told her. He then invited another missionary to join him in anointing Mrs. Hay and commanding the demons to depart.

After prayer, Mrs. Hay went home and threw away all her remaining Buddhistic possessions, regardless of their value. From that time on, she was freed from harassment by the spirits.

One Sunday, Mrs. Hay brought a couple of her friends to church. "They need Jesus," she said. "I have a feeling that I may not be around much longer." The next evening, we received news that Mrs. Hay had had a heart attack and had gone to be with Jesus. She was laid to rest in a cemetery with others who had died in the faith. The message of salvation had come to her "just in time."

One afternoon, Merle and I went to the largest hospital in the city. The daughter of a local pastor had been admitted the previous day, gravely ill. As we drove into the parking lot, I could scarcely hold back my tears. This was the first time that I had visited this particular hospital since our return to Cambodia. It was the hospital where our Marilyn had lain seriously ill with bulbar polio in 1955. God had touched her, and we rejoiced that she was now a missionary serving with her husband, Fred, in Peru. However, Marilyn and Fred had already gone through a difficult trial of their own. Their first child, a daughter, had died and been buried in Mexican soil while they were in language study.

As we entered the hospital, it became obvious to us that the pastor's daughter was near death. More than twenty-four hours had passed since she had been admitted and no doctor had yet been in to see her.

The hospital was crowded with war casualties. Rooms were bulging. Patients occupied beds lined up against the walls of the corridors. Sheets were often blood-stained, and there were no clean sheets available with which to change the beds. Some patients had no sheet at all, and others had no bed, but were lying on the floor. Still others, desperately ill, were turned away and taken from one hospital to another in an attempt to gain entrance.

The pastor's daughter, approximately fourteen years old, had been given a corner in a small room in a back section of the hospital. Her back was stiff, and her throat was apparently paralyzed, for she could utter only unintelligible sounds. Small children were running near her bed. Flies were everywhere—on her food and utensils, crawling on her face and over her body. Her symptoms resembled those that Marilyn had suffered. Doubtless, the girl had meningitis or polio. Greatly moved, we prayed with the girl's mother, who was anxiously keeping vigil.

The following morning, word reached us that the girl had gone to be with Jesus at about 5 a.m. No doctor had yet visited her to even diagnose her illness.

The grim reality of war faced us on every hand. The population of Phnom Penh continued to swell from over 600,000 to 2 million people. Babies and children died every day from disease and malnutrition. Every hospital was full and overflowing; wards were up to double their capacity. War wounded lay on floors, including in aisles and vestibules of hospitals, some minus arms or legs, others with multiple wounds, their lives hanging in the balance. Surgeons sometimes worked all night, then had to discharge patients to find room for the new ones. Those who were unqualified performed emergency operations with inadequate equipment. Medicine was scarce, and even aspirin was sold in lots of only two or three pills at a time. Orphan children roamed the halls because their parents had died and they had no place to go.

Dr. Stanley Mooneyham, then president of World Vision, walked through the charred ruins of a little hospital in the town of Kompong Speu, which had been heavily damaged by the North Vietnamese. Though the hospital had been clearly identified by a red cross, the Vietnamese had entered, stabbed four patients to death, stolen all the medicine, kidnapped two doctors and burned the buildings.

This tragedy prompted Dr. Mooneyham to share his burden with leaders of the Church and mission as well as top-level Cambodian government officials. In response the government offered a ninety-nine-year lease for a hospital to be constructed on twelve acres of the capital's best land located on the main road to the airport. When completed, the 100-bed hospital would be the first Christian medical institution permitted in Cambodia.

Merle served as the representative of World Vision in the Khmer Republic for two years at the same time that he was seeing to his mission responsibilities. He and Dr. Mooneyham worked together with the minister of health on vital issues concerning the hospital. It was an excellent way to contact many of Cambodia's highest officials.

Plans were to construct the new hospital, designed for pediatric care, in two phases. It would be administered and staffed by The Christian and Missionary Alliance. All were excited at the prospect of another hospital.

Dr. and Mrs. Dean Kroh spearheaded the Alliance medical team, and three nurses arrived to assist them. While waiting for the hospital to be erected, the medical team ministered in refugee camps. As they cared for the long line of sick people, others spread out into the camp to visit, witness and distribute gospel tracts. In a period of only one and a half years, four churches were started in the camps where the medical team served.

****

When hundreds of refugees fled to Prek Samrong, there was no clinic or nurse to assist them. Many were sick and needed medicine. Bible school students held children's meetings and church services to give the refugees the message of hope. When the medical team arrived to minister to physical needs, there was no place for them to work. A thatched-roof bamboo building was needed to serve as a clinic, school and chapel.

When a World Vision film photographer heard of the need, he said, "I'll give $100." Some months later, the photographer returned to Cambodia, and the medical team escorted him to Prek Samrong to see the chapel he had helped provide. His heart was deeply touched as he saw what the power of the gospel could do.

But as the enemy pressed nearer to the city, the refugee center was shelled. Once again, the people fled. While I was teaching at the Bible school one morning, refugees began to stream into the compound. When I returned that afternoon, several ladies followed me into the classroom.

"Madam, please give us rice. Our children are hungry."

The Bible school director was a member of the Relief Committee, so I replied, "The director of the school will return shortly and help you."

"But, Madam, our children can't wait. They are hungry."

"You will obtain help soon," I assured her.

Finally, they all filed out of the room except one elderly lady. I can still envision the suffering reflected in her tired, wrinkled face as she looked up into mine and said, "Madam, we have been fleeing with little ones by land and by water. It is so difficult. Madam, I didn't think I could make it."

My heart was deeply moved. Before the day was over, about 250 families—approximately 1,000 people—had flooded onto the school grounds. The students held services nightly for them, and soon more than 100 had prayed for salvation.

As the school choir practiced, refugee youth stood in the classroom doorway and listened. Suddenly, I realized how appropriate was the message we were singing. It was the Cambodian translation of the hymn "Where Jesus Is 'Tis Heaven," and in the Khmer language, the first verse is translated:

> Since Christ forgave my sins,
> This world is like heaven already.
> Through suffering or difficulty,
> If you know Him, you are not afraid.

The impact of the medical team's spiritual ministry was revealed in one testimony. At a refugee camp on the edge of Phnom Penh, the people were asked if they were receiving help from any relief organization. They replied, "Not much, but there is a medical doctor who has been coming to help us. His name is Dr. Kroh. When he doesn't have what we need, he says that he will bring it the next time. And he always keeps his word. He disseminates the Lord."

The number of refugees crowding into reception centers increased daily. The telltale red hair of severe malnutrition was evident among many children. Every night, several would die from diseases related to malnutrition. Burdened with the sight of these homeless and suffering people, church leaders determined to manifest the love of Christ to the refugees. They opened an English language school and used the proceeds for refugee work and evangelism.

Minh Thien Voan, the elder whose name interestingly meant "heavenly messenger," provided excellent leadership as chairman of the relief committee. This evidence of compassion soon opened new doors of witness both among government officials and refugees.

Additional funds from the Alliance constituency and World Vision enabled the Church to assist with thousands of gifts of food and clothing. With every gift, whether a bottle of fish sauce or a package of salt, a tract or a gospel booklet was included. So impressive was their testimony that this little group was called upon frequently by the government to assist in some new area. In one short year, the Church had risen from obscurity to a position of stature.

A government official was heard to remark, "The Christians help in times of need. They give assistance in the hour of desperation. What do our monks do? They beg food from the destitute, making the poor poorer."

On one occasion, the Church was asked to distribute fish oil to 50,000 refugees at a certain center. Fortunately, some money had arrived for relief purposes, so a small truck was filled with supplies. Not only were the accompanying Christians given special escort, but also a huge sign was attached to each side of the car which read "Cambodian Evangelical Church."

Military officers recognized Major Taing Chhirc among the delegation, though he was not dressed in uniform. "Why would you come into such a dangerous area unarmed?" they asked him. Before he could respond, one of them added, "Oh, yes, you have your God to protect you."

Merle wanted to visit the provincial town of Takeo; Tuy Sreng was the pastor the church there. He asked the government for use of a helicopter, and the request was granted. Merle could use it at his discretion for a day. A pilot and a gunner with a full complement of ammunition were also provided.

Accompanying Merle were the mission doctor, a nurse and the national church president. Arriving at Takeo, they were met by the commanding general and the governor of the province. The government had notified them in advance of Merle's coming and a lovely banquet had been prepared.

The population of the town was swelling with refugees who had fled from the countryside. Little makeshift shelters lined the road leading into the town. Our group distributed relief supplies, and the doctor and nurse set up a temporary clinic to examine adults and children who had no other recourse for medical help.

The commanding general gave Merle a personal tour of the town and its outskirts. Deep craters caused by the B-52 bombings pocked the countryside. "If it had not been for the B-52 bombings, this town would have fallen long ago to the communists," the general said. "Please tell this to the American people."

When it was time to go, the helicopter spiraled into the air in a corkscrew pattern to avoid enemy fire. Merle and his group departed, leaving behind a brave pastor and a little band of Christians trusting God for a future that, for now at least, appeared so grim.

14

The Rest of the Story

I stood on the bank of the Bassac River with eyes full of joyful tears. "It's a happy day," exclaimed a prominent lady of the city, a convert of only six months.

The Cambodian churches of the Phnom Penh area had combined for weekend services at the Ta Khmau Bible School. They had begun Saturday afternoon with a youth meeting. It was now noon on Sunday, and we had already been in session for four hours. Six people had prayed for salvation, and a number of Christians had sought God for closer fellowship. A baptismal service was concluding the weekend, and twenty-nine persons committed themselves to follow the Lord during that sacred ordinance, fourteen of whom were Mnong tribesmen.

It was the sight of those Mnong that had brought tears to my eyes. Not long ago, they had lived in hidden villages in the mountains of northeastern Cambodia. Their lives had been filled with superstition, fear and witchcraft. Ed and Ruth Thompson, C&MA missionaries living in Kratie (Kraw-CHEH), Cambodia, had made occasional trips into Mnong territory to take the message of salvation and had returned with stirring stories. Standing by the riverbank after the baptismal service, with the noonday sun casting its blazing rays upon us, I recalled the particular story that had caused such deep emotion to well up within my heart:

One night in 1957, Ed sat in a chief's longhouse in the flickering light of a pitch torch while storytellers entertained him by chanting their ancient tribal lore. Ed was fascinated as they told the story of the creation of the world, the fall of man and the flood. Their version was very similar to the story told in Genesis.

But then the story suddenly stopped, without an ending. "Continue on," Ed urged.

They responded, "Through the years much of this story has been lost or forgotten, and we do not know the rest of the story."

With trembling hands, Ed opened the Bible to the book of Genesis and unfolded the story of creation, of man's fall and of God's plan of salvation through the blood of Jesus Christ, not the blood of water buffaloes.

As nearly a hundred tribesmen sat silently staring, the chief spoke. "Oh, we have wondered ever so long what the rest of that story is. It is such a good story. Please say it once more."

After hearing for the second time, the chief spoke again. "This sounds in our hearts like the very truth. If you will come among us and teach us, we will believe."[1]

In 1963, the president of the National Youth Committee made a trip with the Thompsons to the

Mnong area. When they returned, they brought a Mnong teenager named Bly Den to attend both the National Church Conference and the youth conference. Bly Den accepted Christ and became the firstfruit of the National Youth Committee's work among the Mnong in Cambodia. But since then he had returned to his people, and his fate was unknown.

Ed and Ruth Thompson were martyred in Vietnam in 1968. Northeastern Cambodia became too insecure to obtain government permission for a worker to reside there, and in 1970, as the war spread, many of the tribesmen of Mondolkiri Province fled before the enemy. How excited we had been to learn that a large group, eventually numbering about 3,000, had come to Phnom Penh as refugees and were living on the opposite bank of the Mekong River.

The Cambodian Christians received the Mnong refugees warmly. The national church relief committee manifested love and concern by distributing rice and dried fish. A Sunday school was begun, and the number of new Christians grew. One witch doctor accepted Christ and burned his fetishes. A church was built on a plot of ground in their camp, and there were about 100 believers.

The Cambodian church invited the Mnongs to participate in the combined weekend services. Though their voices were untrained and their tongue foreign to our ears, it was beautiful to hear the familiar strains of "Jesus Loves Me" coming from hearts that had now heard of that love.

Major Y-Nam Eban, second in rank in the tribal refugee settlement, and his family were among the converts. At the next baptismal service, he requested that he and his wife be the first in line. "I am a leader in my camp," he said. "I want to be a spiritual testimony and example to my people." God had brought Mnong tribesmen to our door where they were given the opportunity to hear "the rest of the story."

One Sunday morning a young Raday tribesman, an army officer, visited Bethany Church. He and his family had found Christ while living in Banmethuot (Baan-me-TOO-it), Vietnam. Due to the infiltration of the Viet Cong in their area in 1965, they and many others had fled to the province of Mondolkiri in northeastern Cambodia. In the group were approximately 100 Christians. Though they had no pastor, they continued to meet together each Sunday to read the Scriptures and sing hymns.

As the political situation deteriorated, the men were inducted into the army and the women and children were evacuated to more secure areas. Those who came to Phnom Penh were welcomed and ministered to by the Cambodian Christians.

Merle spoke one Sunday to a little Raday congregation of sixteen adults and twenty children. Due to a battle in progress, some of the men were absent. We met outside in a cemented area with only a simple roof for protection from the sun. A few benches and chairs were in place along with a table covered with an army blanket. An attractive red bag decorated with a cross lay on the table and served as a receptacle for the offering.

Hymns of praise in the Raday tongue had filled the air, a baby had been dedicated to the Lord, two individuals had requested prayer and we had had a good time of Christian fellowship. My heart was truly blessed.

After the service, we were invited into the room that the young officer and his family occupied. As their guests, Merle and I were invited to partake of Pepsi with the host. A cheaper beverage had been prepared for the others. We were then extended an invitation to return at a later date to dine with the officer and his wife.

On our way home, three things came to my mind: First, where we meet is not of utmost importance— it is the sincere worship of the heart that counts; second, life consists not of the abundance of things we possess; and, third, out of poverty, these people had given not only to the Lord but had shared with us also. Like the widow whom Christ commended (see Mark 12:41-44), they had done what they could. We had gone to minister to them, but they had also ministered to us.

Chau Uth, the Cambodian national church president, was serving as pastor at Domdech in the interior of Cambodia. The communists had gained control of that area, and Pastor Uth and his family found themselves isolated in enemy territory. No word had been heard from them for several months.

Then, suddenly, they appeared in Phnom Penh with a story of miraculous deliverance.

[One evening] Pastor Uth closed the shutters of his home and gathered his family together for evening prayers. Since the Communists had taken over his village nearly two years ago, God had wonderfully cared for Pastor Uth and his family. God's peace and protection had been theirs. So far, they could preach the gospel without any restrictions except that of getting permission every two weeks. God had honored their desire that their young children should not be forced to take part in learning to sing communist songs with the other school children. When the neighborhood youngsters were called together to sing, for some unexplained reason their children were not called. As yet, no harm had come to them, but they knew that before long their work would be greatly restricted. They were in a quandary—should they remain in spite of restrictions or should they try to leave? No one was allowed to go legally—they would have to sneak out. For a long time they prayed, asking God for His direction and to provide a way of escape if that was His will.

One evening as the family gathered for prayer they suddenly heard a voice calling from outside, "Kru! Kru!" "Teacher! Teacher!" Strange; it sounded like the voice of Mrs. Ellison (who had served the Lord faithfully as a missionary in Cambodia for many years)! Quickly they opened the shutters and scanned the moonlit yard below. No one was there! Their hearts were filled with awe. What did it mean? Pastor Uth and his wife concluded that this was a sign to them from God that He was calling them out and so they began to make plans to leave.[2]

As president of the national church, Pastor Uth had continued thinking of his responsiblity and had asked the local communist leaders for permission to leave, but their reply was, "When we win the war, you can go." Their departure now would have to be extremely secretive and well-planned in order to avoid suspicion. They would inconspicuously sell their pigs and leave some chickens behind.

Finally the day came, and Pastor Uth took two of his children to a predetermined place, where he left them for the night and would meet with them the following day. He then hired a guide to return with him.

The following morning at 3:30 a.m., he and his remaining family started out on bicycles. He, his wife and one child rode one bicycle; the guide and the other two children rode another. It was common for country people to leave home before daybreak to take produce to market or to go to rice fields, so their early morning activity would not be considered out of the ordinary.

They passed checkpoints, but Pastor Uth had the necessary papers for local travel and they were permitted to continue. At about 7 a.m. they reached their first destination, where they met the other two boys and hired another guide.

It was now necessary for them to separate. Arrangements were made for Mrs. Uth to ride in an ox-cart with daughter Sopani and little Noah. Two of the boys, Joash (nine) and Johan (eleven), were instructed to follow at a distance in the fields as though they were country lads searching for their oxen. Pastor Uth and thirteen-year-old Joel would take another route, cutting through rice fields and bush. They were all to meet that first night at a designated farmhouse.

It is hard to imagine the fear that must have filled Mrs. Uth's heart as the wheels of the oxcart creaked and groaned along the country road. Would she ever see the rest of her family again? The oxcart driver had papers for local travel, but they were outdated, so when they reached a checkpoint, he pled illiteracy. When a soldier checked a small box containing a few of their belongings, not even Mrs. Uth knew that her husband had risked hiding a Bible, a songbook and identity papers therein. In God's providence, the soldier did not check the bottom of the box.

That evening they came into an area where fighting had taken place nearby. As the darkness deepened, the courageous family, who had been miraculously reunited, slipped out to continue their journey. By the following evening they were approaching the town of Siem Reap, where they rested for a couple of days. When they silently resumed their flight in the blackness of night, traversing fields and forests, they did not worry about snakes or wild animals, but rather about being detected by communist soldiers. Mrs. Uth, wearily carrying Noah and leading Sopani, almost stumbled at times. Sopani was ill with a cold, and Mrs. Uth feared that even a slight cough might alert the enemy.

On and on they trudged, stopping at least once at another house to rest. Finally, with indescribable joy and songs of praise they came within sight of their destination! Six different guides had been employed along the way. God had certainly protected and imparted the needed strength.

After enjoying some rest and fellowship with believers in the town of Moung, they left by bus for the city of Phnom Penh. There they were reunited with their oldest daughter, Daly, who had previously escaped, and with Christians who welcomed them with great joy and thanksgiving to God for answered prayer.

Daly was a Bible school student. She had been home on vacation when the communists entered their area. Caught there for more than a year, she decided one day to make plans to escape. Leaving while the fields were still flooded, she had rented a boat to reach a certain village. Her parents had never known whether or not she had arrived in Phnom Penh.

After becoming aware that she was missing, the communists had questioned the parents two or three times, "Where is Daly?"

"She asked permission to leave to obtain work," they replied.

Then the parents heard that the village to which Daly had gone had been invaded. Many had fled to another area. If Daly wasn't at the village, where was she?

When questioned again, the mother replied, "Perhaps she went with the group who fled that area."

What agony must have gripped the parents' hearts as they wondered each day what had happened to their daughter. But what rejoicing when they were all reunited and could share the wonderful testimony of God's faithfulness and guidance in each of their lives!

The national church reelected Pastor Uth as their president, but a few years later both he and his wife would be numbered among that list of faithful martyrs who are now rejoicing around the throne of God.

Notes

1. C. Edward Thompson, "The Rest of the Story." *Cambodia* 3, no. 4, p. 10.
2. Marie Ens, "Deliverance." *World Missions Folio* (Harrisburg, PA: Christian Publications, Inc., September/November, 1974), pp. 89-91.

15

The Great Master Has Come

C hristmas always afforded the Cambodian Christians a special opportunity to share the story of
God's love with the people around them. Churches
were artistically decorated and programs enthusiastically presented.

As Christmas 1971 approached, a new sense of
personal responsibility was gripping the aggressive
young leaders of the Church. They took seriously
the matter of pursuing every avenue within their
means to reach the lost for Christ. Consequently,
they decided to launch a new venture in public
evangelism.

On December 25 the national church rented the
second largest government auditorium in Phnom
Penh for a two-hour Christmas service featuring a
seventy-voice youth choir and a men's quartet. Four
speakers would present different aspects of the
Christmas message. As the program theme they
chose a phrase which, translated into English, states,
"A Great and Powerful Master Has Come."

That idea and those words were already familiar to the populace. Cambodian legend told of a great and powerful Master who would someday deliver the country during a time of war. He would make his appearance at a place called the "Four Faces," the site where the auditorium was located. There the Mekong River briefly joins the Tonle Sap River, then branches off in a southeasterly direction while the Tonle Sap becomes the Bassac River flowing directly south.

According to the legend, the blood of battle would flow as high as the stomach of the elephant. At that time a god would come with scars in his hands, feet and side. This god would be a Sarmatre, a god of peace who would reign for 1,000 years with equality and justice.

Since Cambodians from all walks of life desired to learn about this deliverer, more than 700 people filled the auditorium; among them was at least one government representative who was sent to report who this Great One was. At least 1,500 people were turned away because of a lack of space.

Some time after the Christmas program, Dr. Mooneyham and Merle were riding down a city street with a high-ranking government official who was a personal advisor to President Lon Nol. Dr. Mooneyham turned to Merle and said, "Ask him if we could rent the Moha Srap auditorium for a city-wide crusade."

"No problem," replied the official.

The auditorium, seating 1,200, was provided to us for three days with no rental fee. It was to be the first citywide crusade ever held in Cambodia. Dr. Mooneyham would be the evangelist, and World Vision assumed the responsibility of costs for air conditioning and janitorial services.

How would the citadel of Buddhism react to such public speaking? What would be the reaction of the government? What about security in a city where theater bombings were becoming more frequent? (Some Cambodian officials were genuinely concerned that a bomb would be exploded.) Would there even be sufficient interest to fill an auditorium of such size?

Two thousand beautiful posters and 30,000 handbills were distributed, as well as several hundred personal invitations to government officials and business and professional people. Ads appeared in newspapers for five days. Forty counselors were trained, and the Danniebelles, a well-known American singing group, arrived to provide special music. The theme was "Good News for Cambodia." The theme song, a Cambodian tune with Christian words, was mimeographed to distribute to the audience. What would be the response to all of this effort? We were hardly prepared for what happened.

For security purposes, the government required that military police be on hand to search everyone entering the gate. Because of an evening curfew, the service was scheduled to begin at 4 p.m. At about 2:30, the crowd began to gather. A quick search was made of the building and at 3:05 p.m. the gate was opened.

The military police had not anticipated such a large crowd and were unable to cope with those who surged through. By 3:20 the auditorium was packed and the door locked, with more than 100 people caught between the gate and the door. When they began to pound on doors and windows demanding entrance, Dr. Mooneyham went to the microphone. "Tomorrow," he said, "we will have an open-air service preceding the one inside. Please come back tomorrow." When the people refused to leave, it was agreed that they, and only they, could enter and stand along the sides of the auditorium. An additional 4,000-6,000 people were turned away.

The seventy-voice youth choir opened the service, and the Danniebelles performed. After a simple but pointed message stressing new life in Christ, the question was asked, "Do you want this new life?" Hundreds rose to their feet.

But perhaps they had misunderstood. "Think it over," said Dr. Mooneyham. "You may be mocked, ridiculed, expelled from your home. If you are still interested, please come forward."

Without hesitation, a great number moved to the front. Could they really be serious? After more admonition and prayer, the service was dismissed. Those who had come forward were invited to advance to the platform to receive further counseling, literature and prayer. Even as the crowd moved toward the exits, others came forward. They were divided into groups, their names and pertinent information were recorded and counselors dealt with them further.

The following day, permission was given to erect a platform and install microphones within the fenced area outside the auditorium for the overflow crowd. Approximately 4,000 people filled the enclosure.

"God loves you," Dr. Mooneyham told the crowd. They cheered as though they were hearing wonderful news for the first time. When an invitation was given, so many raised their hands that there were not enough counselors to adequately deal with them.

Inside, the auditorium was again filled, and the doors were again locked one half hour before the service was to start. "How many of you were here yesterday?" asked Dr. Mooneyham. It appeared to be a new congregation. Perhaps those who were turned away the previous day had come early for a seat. Again, many responded to the message and remained for counseling. The third day, the same situation prevailed.

When the crusade ended, it was estimated that 10,000 had attended the meetings. Six hundred fifty-four people had made a decision for Christ and 369 had inquired further concerning Christianity. Ninety percent of those responding were male, the majority being young men of high school and university age. One Cambodian pastor attending the crusade was so amazed that he remarked, "Is this us, or isn't it?" He returned to his city a new and invigorated servant of the Lord.

But the results did not end there. The following Sunday, new converts and inquirers were present in four of the five evangelical churches in the area. One church could not seat all who came. More decisions for Christ were made. There was new hope and en-thusiasm on the part of both pastors and laypeople.

Seven months later, a six-day crusade was held in the same auditorium, and Dr. Mooneyham returned as the evangelist. The populace, tired of war and hungry for peace, was attracted by the theme: "The Way of Peace."

The Palermo brothers, a well-known singing duo who had had a unique ministry with Youth for Christ for more than twenty-five years, came to provide the music. In addition to singing at the crusade, the brothers also performed before 22,000 students in 19 schools and appeared on local television prior to the initial meeting. The local television station oper-ated only two hours each evening. However, that night the brothers were given a forty-minute time slot. Five minutes before the conclusion of their per-formance, President Lon Nol telephoned the station requesting that the brothers continue. They enthusi-astically dedicated a special number to the presi-dent, titled "If God Be for Us, Who Can Be against Us?"

The auditorium was filled each day of the crusade. Dr. Mooneyham clearly set forth the way of peace. "One Way" became the slogan as hundreds of youth each day held up one finger and shouted, "One way!" When the invitations were given, the young people stood *en masse*. An additional service was held on the Bible school compound with an attendance of over 500, including some refugees from a nearby camp. The director of the camp was among those who prayed to receive Christ.

At the conclusion of the seven days, 2,681 people had made a profession of faith and signed a decision card. Small literature packets had been prepared and distributed to all who attended, a different packet for each day.

Follow-up became a major focus of the Church. Attempts were made to contact as many new converts as possible. Several Bible studies per week were begun to instruct them. A correspondence course was offered, and youth rallies were held in different locations. At one such rally, 300 were present, many of whom were brought by new converts, and 60 prayed for salvation and signed a decision card.

In addition to the two citywide crusades, Dr. Richard Harvey had ministered in another series of meetings during which ninety-five accepted Christ. Thus, within a period of 7 months in the 3 evangelistic thrusts, at least 3,430 Cambodians had made a profession of faith.

Perhaps some may ask, "Were they genuine conversions?" Of course, only God knows, but there were indications that many had made sincere and lasting commitments. Merle was asked to teach a class for fifteen baptismal candidates. As he walked into the room, he noticed three young people huddled together having a prayer meeting. "I was saved during the first Mooneyham crusade," one told him.

"I gave my heart to the Lord when Dr. Harvey was here," said another.

"I have found the Christian life so exciting since I met the Lord," said yet another.

"You prayed with me one Sunday to accept Christ," testified one young man.

"My life has been really transformed," said a soldier. "God has already answered prayers for me. I want to serve Him until I die."

Some months later, the Buddhist-oriented government held a youth congress at the same auditorium where the two citywide crusades had been held. The purpose of the gathering was to encourage the 1,000 Cambodian youth who attended to maintain their Buddhist faith in opposition to atheistic communism.

One of the high priests of Buddhism addressed the session. During a question-and-answer period, he was asked why there had been reluctance on the part of Buddhist leaders to grant complete freedom of religion. He replied, "Of all the other religions, only Christianity is good for Cambodia. I have a Bible, and I have read it. I find that Jesus Christ was more than just an ordinary man." He referred to the story in Matthew 22:21 concerning Jesus and the question of allegiance. Jesus had replied, "Give to Caesar what is Caesar's, and to God what is God's." The priest concluded, "No mere human being has that kind of wisdom. Jesus had to be God." Then he added, "Perhaps many of you in this audience believe in Christ. Those who do, please raise your hands."

Approximately half of the audience raised their hands. Many of them had no doubt received Christ previously in that same auditorium. The priest then invited volunteers to come forward and discuss the merits of Christianity, and several responded to the challenge. Amazing! This was a great victory for the gospel.

Another encouragement was a Campus Crusade Lay Training Institute held to train Christians in personal evangelism. Three of their personnel came from Manila. It was the first time that they had held an institute where the attendance increased each day.

On Sunday afternoon, 102 persons went out to share their faith using the little booklet "The Four Spiritual Laws." They were instructed to return by a certain hour and to bring decision cards with the names of those who had prayed.

"We prayed with twelve," reported two young men.

"We prayed with eleven at a refugee camp," announced two others.

"I have brought back the young man who I prayed with," said still another.

"I can't read," said an illiterate woman, "but when I approached someone, I would say, 'This is a wonderful book, but I am not able to read it. Will you read it to me?' "

One of the men did not even return—he wanted to continue witnessing. "It wasn't dark yet," he later said. "I wasn't ready to go back."

New converts, babes in Christ, went out with fear and trembling, but the Lord went with them, honoring His Word and giving them fruit. The group reported a total of 100 decisions for Christ that afternoon.

As the wife of our Bible school director was returning home after a ladies' tea held on the closing day of the institute, she had "The Four Spiritual

Laws" in her hand. An army lieutenant was seated beside her in the *remorque*. Noticing the booklet, he asked, "May I have it?"

"This is my personal copy," she replied, "but if you will come to the Bible school, perhaps you can get one there."

There at the school, the lieutenant prayed to accept Christ and returned to Phnom Penh to attend the closing session of the institute.

As recorded in Acts 2:47 concerning the early Church, so it was in the Khmer Republic: "The Lord added to their number daily those who were being saved."

16

Three Miracles

The power of the gospel is clearly revealed in lives that have been totally transformed, and this is one of the strongest evidences of the truth of the Christian faith. We had the privilege of being eyewitnesses of such miracles in Cambodia.

Sin Sum

Born in the village of Siem Reap, Sin Sum was one of six children raised in poverty by a peasant farmer. As a youngster, he had a desire to become a leader but did not want power. Early in life his world was shattered when he lost a brother and his father. He left home to study in a Buddhist temple and do further formal studies. At the age of twenty-two, he married Kao Long and they set out for the city of Battambang where Sin Sum took a teaching position. Later, he taught agriculture in Kompong Speu.

But Sin Sum's world was about to fall apart again. The Viet Cong moved into his area, terrorizing the villagers, planting land mines and killing the innocent. Since teachers were always an early target, Sin Sum and his family found themselves fleeing as refugees.

He obtained a teaching position in a junior high school in Phnom Penh. The dreams of Sin Sum's boyhood began to fade as he witnessed a failing economy and a government struggling to survive. Then, at the age of thirty-four, he read an advertisement in a newspaper, "Hear the Good News for Cambodia."

Sin Sum was one of those who was turned away on the opening day of the first citywide crusade in Phnom Penh. He had arrived at the auditorium fifteen minutes early only to find an overflow crowd. "You advertised a 4 p.m. meeting and free seating. I demand entrance," he told the guard at the gate. But the door was closed, and Sin Sum walked away irate, muttering aloud to himself.

The following day he arrived early, and this time he found a good seat in the balcony. Dr. Mooneyham, through an interpreter, spoke of Jesus' life, death and resurrection. "Jesus is alive," he proclaimed, "and wants to bring His life and peace to every Cambodian."

Sin Sum listened attentively and trembled. "Everything I heard was new to me," he later testified. "When the invitation was given, I just leaped to my feet. I was the first one to respond." Sin Sum's conversion was genuine and his life completely transformed.

Sin Sum hurried home. He had exciting news to share with his wife, Kao. "I've found the Sarmatre. I have peace!" Three months later, Kao also became a Christian.

"The low salary plus a wife and six children made things difficult for me," Sin Sum testified. "I was often worried, appearing like a man lost and full of fear. I hated the house where I lived. My wife and children did not even dare speak to me. Dr. Mooneyham's words caused me to leave my seat and go forward to submit myself to God. I was invited to go to church every Sunday to study the Bible and pray. Realizing that my sins were gone, I became a loving father and husband, always ready to help and show kindness to others. I no longer have love for pleasure, money or sin. I have a new life with hope. By the Spirit of God, I have been born again."

Now Sin Sum's countenance was always joyful, and he had a contagious smile. The mean man had become a happy one. The rocky marriage was transformed into a beautiful team for God. Sin Sum's witness among his students became so effective that the government transferred him to an administrative position at the school. "Praise the Lord," he said to Merle one day with a smile. "I now have more time to witness for the Lord."

The junior high school where Sin Sum taught was within a mile of the Mnong refugee center. Recognizing the tremendous need for opening that area to the gospel, Sin Sum became a key figure in the construction of a chapel seating more than 200 people.

But Sin Sum was a man with fire in his heart; he could not remain static. As the Mnong believers grew in number, Sin Sum decided that it was time to move on to new territory.

Immediately northwest of the city was an area called New Phnom Penh—a section of land in the northwestern part of the city that was not yet developed. There was no electricity, the closest water supply was a fifteen-minute walk away and shopping was a half-day's journey.

This migration of refugees provided a wonderful opportunity for teaching these people and leading them to the Lord. So, leaving their city home, Sin Sum and Kao joined the refugees and became squatters themselves on this land. First they built a palm-branch hut, but later they built a little wooden house which they dedicated to the service of the Lord. Each Sunday the family moved the furniture out of their home so they could fill it with people eager to enter and hear about forgiveness, peace and hope. The little house was soon filled to capacity.

As the guerrilla forces overran villages, leaving numerous dead among the charred wreckage, the more fortunate trudged, weary and heartbroken, down the road toward what they hoped would be a safer haven. As this homeless stream of humanity arrived at New Phonm Penh, Sin Sum and Kao were there to welcome them to "God's Place."

"We have been running for over three years," said one of the refugees. "This is the first time that we have heard about Jesus. He has calmed our fears and brought peace to our hearts."

The church relief committee met the refugees' urgent needs by building temporary shelters for the people as well as providing food, clothes and other essentials. Sin Sum held several Bible classes weekly. As guns roared in the background and the refugees trembled with fear, Sin Sum would share the truths of Psalm 91, telling them that there is a Friend who would watch over and protect them. As the number of Christians multiplied, World Vision provided funds to build a church, which was named Horeb (Mount of God).

With a burning passion for souls, Sin Sum followed refugees to yet another camp, where a large group conversion took place and many faithfully followed the Lord.

In an interview with Sin Sum one day, David Longe, director of communications for World Vision of Australia, asked him this question: "When you were a boy, you wanted to be a leader. Do you still want that?"

"My every dream is fulfilled right now," Sin Sum replied. He had found his fulfillment in leading his people to Christ.[1]

Son Sonne

Son Sonne was born of Cambodian parents in the Khmer-speaking section of South Vietnam. There he obtained his secular education, including eight years of study in a Buddhist temple. He had an uncle who was a high priest, and his parents had hoped that Son Sonne would also serve in the priesthood.

Searching for the truth, Son Sonne asked his uncle about sin, acts of merit and heaven. His uncle replied that it was not necessary for Son Sonne to be a monk, so he left the temple at the age of sixteen. Approximately three years later, he went to Phnom Penh to seek work.

Son Sonne's first contact with the gospel was in 1960 when he was invited to attend a church service. Two years later, he renewed a friendship with a young man who was active among the church youth.

Son Sonne began to attend services and received a Bible. He read the book of Proverbs and was impressed by the great wisdom he found in it.

Meanwhile, Son Sonne had become engaged to a young girl of Cambodian-Chinese ancestry. They discussed Christianity, and she began to attend the services also. On Christmas Day, 1962, they both put their faith in Christ. The following March they were married.

One day, Son Sonne and his wife went with a Christian friend to visit the Bible school. Feeling the need to understand God's Word, they wished that someday they could have the opportunity to study there. For a while they prayed about that, but as time passed, they forgot about it. Son Sonne had a good position with a tractor company where he zealously witnessed to all of his fellow workers. When opportunity permitted, he would retreat to the stockroom and pray that God would open the hearts of those to whom he was witnessing.

Then one day his employer informed Son Sonne that his services were no longer needed. He learned that the reason for the abrupt dismissal was his bold witnessing. He tried to find another job, but nothing seemed to open up. Then, one day as Son Sonne was praying, the Lord reminded him of the prayers he had offered several months previously. The Holy Spirit seemed to whisper, "Now is the time to go to Bible school."

So, one autumn day in 1963, Son Sonne and his young bride arrived at the Ta Khmau Bible School one month after classes had begun. "We have sold most of our earthly possessions," he said. "I want to burn every bridge behind me so there will be no temptation to go back." Son Sonne would later serve as the interpreter for the citywide crusades in Phnom Penh.

Two years later, in 1965, while working one day in the church bookroom, Son Sonne was arrested and imprisoned. He chose to suffer rather than stop preaching and teaching about Jesus Christ. Nearly three months later, he was released.

The only Cambodian church in the city had been closed due to government restrictions and pressure, and there were no public services. Son Sonne and his family moved into the building and invited other Christians to come and join them. Gradually the Christians began to reassemble for public services. Soon the group was again large enough to have a pastor, and one was called. That congregation eventually mothered two other churches in 1971.

Son Sonne went on to become director of the United Bible Societies in the Khmer Republic (Cambodia). He was an excellent speaker and frequently occupied a pulpit in one of the churches. Until his schedule became too heavy, he also taught in the English school sponsored by the national church. During just one month in 1972 he led thirty of his students to the Lord and then conducted Bible classes for several weeks to strengthen them in the faith.

He was also president of the Foreign Missionary Society of the Khmer Evangelical Church (C&MA), a member of the relief committee, chairman of the radio committee and a member of the translation committee. He frequently served as language interpreter for foreign guest speakers.

A young man came to Son Sonne one day. He wanted to start a Bible study in his home, and he asked Sonne to be the teacher. There were thirteen present at the first meeting. "Invite your friends," Son Sonne urged the group. They responded, and conversions multiplied until approximately 1,600 people in that area had prayed for salvation.

One evening there was a knock on Son Sonne's door. When he opened it, there stood a teenage girl. "May I pray to become a Christian?" she asked.

Son Sonne was astonished. He did not know the girl nor had he ever witnessed to her. "Why did you come to me?" he asked.

"One day, I listened as you witnessed to a young man," she replied. "I liked what I heard. Now I have decided to become a Christian."

With great delight, Son Sonne led the girl to the Lord. Though the young man had not yet accepted Christ, fruit had come from Son Sonne's witnessing to him. The Lord had skillfully molded a vessel to use for His glory among the Khmer people.

Men Ny Borin

A sleek, black, chauffeur-driven Mercedes pulled up in front of Bethany Church and out stepped a stately and immaculately dressed man. He entered the church and walked down the aisle. Merle recognized the man—he had gone to his home the previous day and invited him to come to the service.

Finding a seat in the second row of chairs, the man listened intently as guest speaker Stanley Mooneyham proclaimed the gospel. When the invitation was given, Men Ny Borin, president of the Supreme Court of the Khmer Republic, was among those who responded. There at the altar he humbly confessed his sins to Jesus Christ.

As a young lawyer, Men Ny Borin had purchased a Bible to find out more about this Jesus Christ of whom he had heard. Then, because of his reputation for integrity, he was appointed to a judgeship. He had always kept the Bible displayed on his desk. It contained, he believed, the right principles for judging. Subsequently, he had received the top justice appointment.

Now, having realized that his own goodness could not save him, but only the blood of Jesus Christ, Men Ny Borin left the church a changed man. He later gave this testimony:

> My life is like the match and the candle. The Bible is the match that finally came in contact with my life which is the candle. Now I feel like a torch, and I want to go around lighting candles. I love my fellow Cambodians more since I know the Lord. I pray that they will find the peace that I have found. My nation is far from God, and much trouble has come because of this fact. I pray that my countrymen will find true peace even during this time of trouble.

This burning torch immediately began to go around lighting other candles. During those days, thousands of refugees were fleeing the countryside to the Phnom Penh area. Normally, high-ranking government officials did not mingle with those of lower position, especially refugees. But the chief justice gave no thought to his earthly position. He frequently went with other Christians to minister to the multitude of displaced persons. He enjoyed sharing his faith with anyone and everyone.

On one occasion, he said to Merle, "Pray for me. I am going to share my faith with the president of my country."

A couple of weeks later he reported, "I shared Jesus with my president. I said to him, 'Mr. President, I have become a Christian. I urge you to trust Jesus Christ as your personal Savior also. Only Jesus Christ can save our nation. You seek advice from fortune tellers and false teachers, but you must receive guidance from the living God.' "

Regretfully, the president did not receive Christ, and the Khmer Republic eventually fell. Meanwhile, Men Ny Borin followed the Lord in baptism and continued in the faith. His torch burned to the end until it was snuffed out by an evil regime.

Note

1. David Longe, "Born to Lead." *Cambodia Update* (Monrovia, CA: World Vision, July/August, 1973).

17

The Grim Reality of War

Bursting bombs, exploding grenades, the rattle of machine guns, rockets, reverberating earth, barbed wire, sandbags, blackouts, curfews—all were concrete evidence that we were in a country at war.

Breakdowns of aging equipment, difficulty in obtaining needed parts for repairs, fire and overload all contributed to a serious shortage of electricity in Phnom Penh. Water pressure was often very low, and rice, the Cambodians' main staple, was in short supply. Food prices were rising and inflation was soaring. In the center of the city, shutters on shops were rolled down by late afternoon. Streets were deserted after the curfew hour.

Flares illuminated the sky, and low-flying aircraft strafed the enemy on the opposite side of the river. Rockets and mortars broke the silence of the night, and residents tried to determine whether the shots were incoming or outgoing.

It was a Friday afternoon in March 1972. Merle and I were having lunch when, suddenly, a loud blast was heard to the north. As we found out later, the communists had tried to destroy the city's only bridge across the Tonle Sap River. The bridge had been constructed by the Japanese as a war reparation after World War II.

Three men had driven onto the bridge in a small French-made truck loaded with firewood. At the middle of the bridge, they stopped. Pretending that the truck would not start, the men began walking away. Moments later, the truck blew up. Apparently a large amount of plastic explosives had been buried both in the engine compartment and under a load of firewood. The blast tore a hole thirty yards wide in the northern half of the center span, weakening the southern half of the bridge and blowing away some of the railing.

Debris was scattered for hundreds of meters. At least one soldier died at the scene, a civilian riding a motorbike was killed instantly and four other civilians were seriously wounded. Fortunately, the three men from the truck were reported captured.[1]

Approximately six months later, I was awakened around 2:30 a.m. by the noise of battle. I listened. It was coming closer, and I was alone. Merle had flown to the seaport town of Kompong Som. What should I do? Was the enemy finally making good on its threat of marching into the city?

I got out of bed and went to the apartment of nurse Mary Lou Rorabaugh. Together we listened and waited until it appeared that the enemy was being contained. Later, we learned what had taken place.

For several days, highly trained communist commandos had reportedly hidden directly across the Tonle Sap River from Phnom Penh. In the predawn darkness that morning, sappers had strapped plastic charges to their bodies and blown the bridge into the water, collapsing it at two points.

As the charges were detonated, momentarily illuminating the night sky, commando units infiltrated the capital and stormed an adjacent sports stadium housing several M113 Armored Personnel Carriers (APCs). Tossing satchel charges and peppering the camp with small arms and bazooka fire, they destroyed five of the vehicles and roared out of the arena with five others. Caught by surprise, a number of civilians and more than fifty government troops were said to have died. One commando unit took refuge on the grounds of the French Embassy. Bullets flew and hysterical civilians in the area fled until the commandos were finally driven out.

As the APCs roared around the foot of the destroyed bridge attempting to head north on Highway 5, government troops rallied more reinforcements and blew up four of the carriers. The fifth was knocked out farther up the road.

By the time it was over, an estimated fifty or more commando corpses littered the roads at the northern end of Phnom Penh. The following day, they lay displayed in open view at the foot of the bridge.[2]

En route to the Bible school every day, we had to pass a military checkpoint and present identification. One morning, as Merle and I neared that area, we noted a long line of traffic backed up along the road.

"What's the problem?" Merle asked of another stranded motorist.

"Rebels infiltrated the area," the man replied. "Government troops are searching the neighborhood to see if any remnants remain."

We later learned that approximately 100 guerrillas had entered Phnom Penh in an attempt to blow up the city's only bridge across the Bassac River. Though the guerrillas had been repelled after considerable fighting, at least 28 people were left dead and 135 others were wounded.

Another night at 2 a.m. thunderous explosions suddenly broke the silence and shook our bed. We dashed to the window. Rockets were raining down on the northwestern section of the city. The sky turned brilliant red as flames from hundreds of recently constructed refugee homes shot into the night sky. Pre-dug trenches under these homes became human incinerators as people tried to take refuge from falling timbers. It was not uncommon to find several bodies, charred beyond recognition, in one trench.

The following afternoon, Merle and I walked through the smoldering ashes where survivors were searching for any remaining possessions. A man stood alone at the site where his home had been. Brokenhearted, he said, "I have lost everything, my home, my family. I have nothing left."

Farther down the path, four bamboo poles stuck up from the ground over which had been placed a simple thatched roof for protection from the sun. Underneath sat a grief-stricken wife. Beside her lay her dead husband, who had a gaping hole in his side. A container had been placed near the body for donations. One hundred forty people were reported killed in the attack and approximately 300 were wounded.

On February 11, 1974, in the middle of the afternoon, more than seventy rounds of highly explosive shells and rockets poured into a densely populated area of the southern part of the city. A mile-square area was in flaming ruins, and entire families had died in the rubble. The wounded lay bleeding on cots in hospital hallways. Plasma and medical supplies were running low.[3]

Two hours after the shelling, residents who had managed to escape returned to dig through the smoldering remains. Some cried hysterically; others were numbed into silence by the spectacle.

"All my family has disappeared," sobbed one woman. "I don't know where to find them. I had eight children. My husband is gone also. I have nothing left, only the clothes on my body."

A group of young girls cried as they stood at the ruins of their home. "This is the fourth time in four years that our home has been burned to the ground," one said.

But in the midst of tragedy, there was a miracle. While fires licked away at the remaining timbers, spreading quickly through the fragile wooden houses clustered closely together, two homes where Christians lived still stood among the ruins, a testimony of divine protection. The wind had twice changed course, and the flames had bypassed those two houses.

As people ran in every direction, fleeing from the indescribable destruction, fear was running rampant.

Amid this utter confusion, a troop of Boy Scouts could be seen. Who were these young men? It was discovered that this particular troop were Christians. They were fearlessly ministering in the time of need. Government officials were amazed and praised the scouts' courage and compassion.

As battered government posts were overrun and casualties continued to rise, wives and mothers anxiously awaited news of husbands and sons in the military. One soldier's wife heard that her husband had been seriously wounded during a battle in another province. For five days she and her seven children had been keeping vigil at one of the hospitals in Phnom Penh, watching the medivac helicopters arrive with war casualties. Her husband was not among them.

Other women also waited. Surrounded by their children, they squatted silently within sight of the landing pad. As the whir of a helicopter approached, they raced to see if wounded husbands or sons were among the passengers. Those more fortunate were airlifted out, but some of the wounded had to come by boat, meaning it would be many hours or even days before they arrived for treatment. It was not uncommon for wives and children of the soldiers to frequently follow the soldiers to their assigned areas, allowing themselves to be subject to the enemy's attacks.

A Christian mother longed for news of her eldest son. Having heard nothing concerning his whereabouts for eight months, she decided to make an effort to find him. Following clue after clue, she eventually learned where his unit was operating. Then, taking a bus to his area, she observed that most of the houses had been burned and only ashes remained. The woman finally found her son. Out of 800 soldiers who had been engaged in a recent battle, her son was one of only 100 who had survived.

As the enemy pressed closer, tightening the noose around Phnom Penh, residents naturally felt an uneasiness about when and where the next round of whining rockets would rain down.

One afternoon Merle and I were working in the mission office when, suddenly, a rocket whizzed by directly overhead. It fell two blocks beyond us, destroying the side of a brick home. Another rocket followed in the same path and fell one block short of us, killing three persons and wounding sixteen.

Each missionary had his or her special assignments or responsibilities. One Sunday, five of us were scheduled to minister in five different churches. As Merle and I were preparing to leave for our assignments, a series of explosions could be heard. Merle was planning to speak to the congregation that met in the Bible school chapel. I was going to Bethany Church to play the organ as I customarily did. But, we wondered, was it wise for couples to separate in the midst of such uncertainty? We decided to go ahead with our plans.

As I rode along in the *cyclo,* the explosions were loud and frequent. Smoke billowed into the distant sky. Arriving at the church, I learned that an ammunition depot had been targeted.

As I was playing the prelude, a heavy blast shook the wall near the organ. I glanced at the words of the hymn. It was one of my favorites.

> All the way my Savior leads me,
> What have I to ask beside?
> Can I doubt his tender mercy
> Who through life has been my guide?
> Heavenly peace, divinest comfort,
> Here by faith in Him to dwell;
> For I know whate'er befall me,
> Jesus doeth all things well.
> For I know whate'er befall me,
> Jesus doeth all things well.[4]

It is the knowledge of His presence that brings peace and tranquillity to the heart in such an hour.

For nearly five years (1970-1975), missionaries traveled over potentially dangerous streets and roads. They shopped for food and necessities in market areas where grenades were sometimes thrown. They went freely to churches where bombs could easily have been placed. They lived in homes that had no armed guards at the gate. Rockets sometimes whizzed over or landed nearby, yet not one was harmed. This was indeed a miracle and an answer to the prayers of all those who were faithful to intercede for us.

Notes

1. "Huge Blast on Bridge," *The Nation*, March 25, 1972, n.p.
2. "Nightmare That Began in Phnom Penh Murky Waters," *Bangkok Post*, October 9, 1972, p. 2.
3. "139 Killed in Shelling of Phnom Penh," *Bangkok Post*, February 13, 1974, n.p.
4. Fanny Crosby, "All the Way My Savior Leads Me," *Sing Joyfully* (Carol Streams, IL: Tabernacle Publishing Co., a division of Hope Publishing Co., 1989), p. 481.

18

Faithful Witnesses

"I have brought someone with me to church this morning. At the conclusion of the service, he is going to accept the Lord."

This testimony was frequently heard at Bethany Church, and as soon as an invitation was given, that person indeed responded. He had made the decision before coming because of the faithful witness of a friend or relative.

Opportunity was also given each Sunday for testimonies. New converts were eager to share their good news. They told of miracles, healings and answered prayers. With simple faith, they believed that God was able to handle any circumstance.

"I have been saved for two months and twenty days," a young man named Somal testified one morning. "When I was in third grade, I had a very difficult time with numbers. The teacher threatened to punish me if I did not remember my numbers. He would give us three or four chances, then punish us until we gave the right answer.

"One day he made me stand at the blackboard with arms outstretched and said, 'I'm going to crucify you like they crucified Jesus.' I didn't understand what he meant. Who was Jesus? I didn't know. Then one day I learned who Jesus was and that He had been crucified on a cross for me."

Somal rejoiced that he now knew Jesus as his Savior and friend.

Young people who accepted Christ often found their parents unsympathetic, especially when they were the first in the family to break away from Buddhist tradition. Chan Sokha gave his heart to the Lord during the second citywide crusade, and he immediately had a problem. Whenever he planned to attend a church service or activity, his mother would hide his clothes. Sokha soon learned to solve the problem by hiding his clothes before his mother could do so.

Sokha also wanted a Bible, but he had no money. He learned that if he sold Bibles, he could earn enough money to purchase one for himself. His first selling attempt was with the Cambodian military. "I was frightened," he said. "I thought they might shoot me." But, fortunately, they were not angry. In due time, Sokha had both a Bible and a hymnal of his own.

Sokha's father drank and sometimes mocked and beat Sokha because of his faith. "You don't believe your own religion. Why believe another?"

Sokha replied, "I believe this one because I have been saved from my sins."

He continued to attend services in the church, including Bible studies, several times a week. Sokha's father died, but his mother still made life difficult.

Anxious to share his faith with his neighbors, Sokha would sit by an open window and read the Word of God aloud. Agitated, the neighbors would rattle pots and pans to distract him and drown out the sound of his voice. One day as Sokha was reading the Bible aloud, his mother came and sat down near him and listened.

The youth group at Bethany Church began an eighteen-hour prayer chain from 6 o'clock in the morning until midnight. They assigned each youth a prayer time so that someone would be praying each hour. "Give us the names of unsaved parents and friends that you would like to place on the prayer chain," suggested the leader. Sokha gave his mother's name. The following week she came to church, prayed for salvation and cut the devil string from her body.

"I am so happy," testified Sokha. "I can't remain quiet. I have to praise the Lord."

Pok Saung, a young man who worked for a shipping company, was always smiling. One Saturday morning his boss asked him to go on an errand to the Immigration Office. Saung went, but before leaving the office, he witnessed to a young female employee. "There is no hope outside of Christ," he told her.

As Saung was leaving the Immigration Office on his motorbike, a rocket came in, demolishing his bike and killing him. His body was burned almost beyond recognition. Just then, one of our missionaries passed by and took a picture, not realizing who it was. The next day, when Saung was not at church, people began to wonder where he was. No one had seen him, and his family did not know where he was; he had not returned home that night.

Then Saung's boss told about the errand to the Immigration Office and how Saung had not returned to work. The missionary told of the picture he had taken, and the Christians began to piece together the events of the previous day. Finally, a relative identified Saung's motor bike, and then they found his body at the morgue.

A memorial service was held at the church. The girl to whom Saung had witnessed at the office, as well as several others, gave their hearts to Christ at the service. God was glorified both in Saung's life and in his death.

The Lord often revealed Himself in unique ways to these new converts. One of them, a young man, prayed one Sunday morning at Bethany Church. The following Tuesday night, he was awakened by a rocket landing in his area. Frightened and shaken, he finally fell asleep again and had a dream. In the dream, it appeared to be dusk. As shadows fell, he saw the form of someone on a cross. Then the scene brightened, and he saw a cross on either side of the first one. At the foot of the cross in the middle, many people were kneeling. Among them were Cambodians.

The next day, the young man went to the home of one of the elders. "Is there anything in the Bible like this that I have seen?" he asked.

The elder told the young man the story of Jesus' crucifixion and the two thieves hanging on either side. The young man was excited. Soon afterward, he shared his testimony at the church.

A new convert visited a hospital in Kompong Chhnang. Among the many patients was a lady who was very ill and whose eyesight was blurred. Responding to the woman's need, the young man knelt and prayed for her. Those who saw him assumed that he had sorcery powers and would want to get some incense sticks to burn.

"I need no incense sticks," he said. "I am praying in the name of Jesus Christ." Confident of an answer to his prayer, he asked the woman, "Can you see now?"

"My eyes feel better," she answered, "but they are not clear yet." So the young man prayed again, and again those nearby wanted to get incense sticks to burn.

"I have no supernatural powers myself," he replied. "Only God can do miracles." Again he asked the woman, "Are your eyes better now?"

"Yes," she replied.

The people were amazed. "We wish there was a church here at Kompong Chhnang so we could go and learn about Jesus too," they said.

Ung Davy was a schoolteacher. After receiving Christ as his Savior, he felt the call of God to full-time Christian service. But what could he do? He had much opposition from his parents, and local authorities were unwilling to release him from his job. So he appealed to the minister of education. As he went from office to office, he was asked, "Why do you want to quit your job? Are you dissatisfied with the government? Is it for political reasons?" These questions always gave him an opportunity to witness. Three teacher friends came to Christ, as did his mother and some of his siblings.

Finally, by faith in God for his support, Ung Davy was able to enter Bible school. One Saturday, he and a few other students went out witnessing. While Davy stood talking to three men, a deadly cobra suddenly appeared in front of them with its head raised to strike. Then it turned and crawled away. "I thought that I might have been in heaven today," he later testified. "But the Lord spared my life for a while longer."

In 1973, the Cambodian church commissioned Davy to go to Europe for further study. There he met and married a young Swiss teacher. Then in 1978, just as they were beginning a ministry among Cambodian refugees in France, we heard the shocking news that both Davy and his wife had been killed in a car accident. In one of their last prayer letters, Davy had written, "When God begins something in our lives, he will carry it on until it is finished on the day of Jesus Christ." Davy's short ministry was finished. We felt privileged to have been among his teachers at the Ta Khmau Bible School.

Nhem Sokun was a commercial artist at the Ministry of Information. He became a Christian about one month prior to the opening of the Bible school in the fall of 1973. Sokun applied for admission to the school but was turned down by the committee. They felt that, as a new convert, Sokun needed more time to prove himself.

Not to be dissuaded, Sokun went to one of the elders at Bethany Church and said, "I feel the call of the Lord. Can you intercede for me?"

The Bible school committee reconsidered and admitted Sokun. He had no money. His father was dead. Being the eldest son, he was expected to assist his mother. He was also the only Christian in his family. Nevertheless, Sokun determined to remain in school and follow the Lord's call. By selling Christian books and literature, he was able to obtain some money to look after his mother.

Sokun survived the holocaust in Cambodia and fled, becoming one of the many refugees to arrive safely at the Khao-I-Dang refugee camp in Thailand. There God used his evangelistic and organizational gifts to bring into existence a church of many thousands.

Sokun eventually went to live in the United States, and several years later he became ill and went to be with the Lord.

From the battlefronts came dramatic accounts of God's deliverance of Christian soldiers from the jaws of death. One soldier told of living on leaves and fruit for twenty days during his escape when, at times, he was within thirty feet of the Viet Cong rebels. Others vividly described having been harbored in the safety of God's protection from exploding shells and other dangers surrounding them.

Following are excerpts from an unpublished article Merle wrote based on the testimony of Van Sonn, a young soldier who enthusiastically declared that God not only granted him a second life but, more important, saved the souls and lives of more than a dozen fellow soldiers faced with sure death.

> From 12 o'clock midnight until 7 o'clock in the morning, we were attacked by many Viet Cong. They were employing large weapons and destroying everything about us, including the pigs and chickens. I prayed and exhorted the others to call upon God in true sincerity. Those who trusted in Buddhism and fetishes were falling all around me but, to my amazement, large shells falling near me were not exploding. At that time, two or three other soldiers sought God when, suddenly, more large shells fell right beside us but did not explode. This was the power of God manifested very clearly to us.

> Simultaneously, others were calling, "Sonn, Sonn, help us."

> I yelled, "I can't help you, but cry out to the Lord Jesus, the true God, and He will save you."

> Three yards further, a shell fell in their midst. I ran and called out again, "Put your trust in the Lord. No one else can help you now."

> Immediately, they cried out in earnest, "Jesus Christ, our Savior, please forgive us, save us and take our spirit with You. Please give our families peace and help them to trust in You."

> At 7 o'clock in the morning, we still had no hope of escape. . . . A loud shot rang out about

thirty yards away, and I fell to the ground slightly wounded.

God said, "Arise and run." He gave me unusual strength to run to a bunker used by the citizens of the area. Upon arriving, I fell unconscious into the bunker.

As I was regaining consciousness, I heard the people within say, "Trust in whatever god is yours."

I exclaimed, "Thank God, I trust in Jesus Christ who has helped me."

They inquired, "Who is Jesus Christ?"

I explained to them briefly and exhorted them to believe likewise. They confessed their sins before the Lord, but I was not able to stay with them.

Sonn escaped with his life and was a constant testimony for the Lord. He subsequently led some of his family as well as others to Christ.

In the midst of war, God was revealing His saving grace and protecting power to the people in Cambodia.

19

When Blood Flows

Anniversaries normally call for joyful celebrations, especially when they are golden ones,
and the year of 1973 marked the fiftieth anniversary
of our mission in Cambodia. But instead of ban-
quets and celebrations, we were holding prayer
meetings and managing strenuous schedules filled
with ministering to the needs of suffering people.

The seed that had been sown for decades and watered through faithful intercession was finally yield-
ing a great harvest. God's promise given in Psalm
126:5-6 was being fulfilled: "Those who sow in tears/
will reap with songs of joy./ He who goes out weep-
ing,/ carrying seed to sow,/ will return with songs of
joy,/ carrying sheaves with him."

We were witnessing in the Cambodian people an
unsatisfied hunger for reading material, a tremendous desire to learn and a search for truth and reality. Many of them also had a great desire to learn
English. As one young man said, "The two most attractive things in Cambodia today are the English
language and Christ."

A professor from the Buddhist university was teaching English to employees of the National Bank, and one day he contacted Merle. "Would you be willing to teach conversational English once a week?" he asked.

At first Merle declined. He was already teaching English twice a week to a Cambodian general who was the personal physician of Marshal Lon Nol, the president of Cambodia. But, after thinking it over and realizing the potential for witnessing to such influential people, Merle replied, "I will do it if I am permitted to use *Good News for Modern Man* as the foundation for our conversation and each student purchases his own personal copy." The professor agreed, and Merle's new class began to meet during the siesta hour.

Then Merle was invited to teach an advanced conversational English class at the Buddhist university. He thought of his Bible classes and speaking schedule. He was already overloaded—how could he possibly take on another English class? But what an opportunity to share Christ with the Buddhist monks! After considerable persuasion, Merle agreed to teach, providing he would be permitted to use the Bible at three out of the four weekly sessions. The university agreed.

At the beginning of Merle's final week of teaching for the school year, one monk said to him, "Please spend this last week just telling us about Jesus."

Another added, "Do you remember that you promised us some Bibles?"

"Yes, I remember," replied Merle, "but there are no more Bibles in the country. More are being printed in Hong Kong."

Then Merle thought about the Gideons. Explaining the Gideon ministry to the monks, he asked them, "Would you like to have a distribution here on Friday?"

"Yes," was their quick reply.

After the monks had received their beautiful red New Testaments, they asked, "Mr. Graven, may we have our picture taken with you while we are holding our New Testaments?"

Their eagerness to receive God's Word and their unhesitating acceptance of a missionary were totally amazing!

One day I was driving to the Bible school alone. I was well on my way after having passed the military checkpoint when I noticed a *remorque* with several passengers approaching from the opposite direction. Suddenly, a young man on a motorbike attempted to pass the *remorque*. Seeing my car and realizing that he could not complete the pass, he tried to make a quick U-turn in my lane. Before my eyes, the bike skidded and the man fell to the pavement. I braked hard and finally stopped. I could see neither the young man nor his bike. Was he under my car? Was he dead or seriously injured? The questions raced through my mind at lightning speed.

There were a number of witnesses at the scene, and I was worried, because I had heard that foreigners are sometimes mobbed in the event of a death.

Despite those fears and not considering my own safety, I immediately got out of the car and walked to the front of it, fearful of what I might find.

To my relief, the young man was getting up from the pavement, seemingly uninjured. "I'm so glad that you are alive!" I exclaimed.

It apparently pleased the young man that I had been concerned about him. Turning to those who had witnessed the accident, he repeated what I had said. Then with an embarrassed grin, he picked up his damaged bike and walked away.

God had marvelously protected us both in a situation that could have ended in tragedy.

God displayed the same wise guidance on another occasion when a Christian colporteur was trying to hire a taxi to bring him to Phnom Penh from Battambang.

"This one is full," one driver told him. "You will have to wait for the next one." The colporteur was disappointed, but he soon learned how God's hand had guided him even in his disappointmnent. He later learned that four taxis and a bus that had gone before him were all stopped by the rebels. His taxi, which left later, had been able to get through without incident.

The Defense Department of the United States announced that US bombing in the Khmer Republic would cease on August 15, 1973. As the date approached, most of the world waited, as it were, with bated breath. Many Cambodians believed that with

the cessation of US bombing the Cambodian government would soon collapse. Months before, a magazine
article had already labeled Phnom Penh "The Dead
City."

"No one loves us but Christians," remarked one
man. "The world is waiting for us to die."

During the month of June, the reverberations of exploding bombs had become more and more a regular
part of both night and daytime noises. For the inhabitants of Phnom Penh, the sound of B-52s and phantom
jets roaring in the skies meant that highways and the
river route might be kept open for convoy supplies and
that the enemy could be held back.

Then, just as the missionary children prepared to
come home for vacation, we were advised by the
American Embassy that we should not bring them
into Cambodia. Further, all dependents—wives and
children—were twice advised to leave the country.
However, since school was scheduled to reopen
early in August, the children would be back in Malaysia before the bombing ceased, so we decided to
bring the children back into Phnom Penh.

Then a telegram arrived from Dalat School, in-
forming us that, since a number of teachers and staff
were awaiting the visas necessary for them to enter
Malaysia, the opening of the school would be post-
poned until August 13. Soon after that a third advi-
sory came: Women and children should depart in
case the airport was closed and commercial flights
became unavailable.

So, two days later, on July 27, four missionary mothers left Cambodia with the ten school children. We left

our homes just as they were, hoping to return as soon as possible. Within a few days, the remaining women and children departed, leaving the five men alone.

We evacuated to Bangkok, Thailand, but shortly after our arrival, we received a wire from Dalat School requesting three of us to come and assist until the regular personnel arrived. So, on August 6 we flew to Penang, Malaysia. My assignment was to teach several subjects in the sixth grade and to supervise a couple of high school study halls.

The beautiful tropical island of Malaysia afforded a welcome but temporary reprieve from the sights and sounds of war in Cambodia. Gazing out across the tranquil water reminded me of a picturesque scene from a lovely postcard. The five weeks we were there passed quickly.

Meanwhile, in the last hours of the US bombing, Phnom Penh was rocked by almost continuous explosions as aircraft bombed rebel forces surrounding the capital. As a youth conference convened at the Bible school, students counted the bombs as they dropped from the planes across the river. Fifteen minutes before the bombing ceased, two American jet fighters streaked over Phnom Penh, apparently bidding farewell to the city they had helped to defend in the past months.

Four days later, a campaign of terror began to rain down on the populace. Three explosions ripped through the center of the city, one only three feet from a military post. The other two shattered the insides of two theaters less than a mile apart. A total of nine were left dead and over forty were wounded.

The government reported that up to 1,000 rebel infiltrators had penetrated the city. Several caches of arms and explosives were discovered. Leaflets, distributed by insurgent supporters, appeared on the streets; they listed eight points on what to do when the armed forces of the National Liberation of Cambodia marched in. They assured the populace that, if orders were obeyed, no one would be harmed.

Enemy forces loosely surrounded the city and militarily controlled an estimated eighty percent of the countryside. To the east of our home, they had infiltrated to within a mile; only the Mekong River separated us. Four thousand insurgents were reported to be massed for an attack on the airport.

Phnom Penh did not fall when American bombing ceased, as had been feared. Most of the children were safely at Dalat School, and in September we missionary women returned to resume our work for as long as possible. But what did the future hold? It was a troubling question.

The Cambodian people have a proverb that says, "When blood flows, the heart grows softer." Certainly war and despair had brought a great yearning for peace and hope among the people. Several city churches were now filled to capacity. A second morning service was begun at Bethany, where an average of five to fifteen were accepting Christ weekly. The elders initiated a period of prayer and fasting on Sunday following the morning worship service, and some gathered daily at 6 a.m. for prayer before going to work.

The fighting was again edging closer to the city. In December, the American Embassy advised all dependents to evacuate. The school children were due for Christmas vacation, and despite the embassy's warnings, we decided to bring the children home.

One day, a telegram arrived. Merle's father had terminal cancer and was nearing death. Since Merle was the only child in the family, it seemed only right that he should go home to see his father and assist his mother with funeral arrangements. Our home assignment was due the following summer, but Merle's father would not be there to greet us.

Merle was faced with a difficult decision. As director of the mission, he felt responsible for being on hand in such a critical hour. He was also fearful of leaving Gordon and me in the city alone. I encouraged him to go and promised that after missionary allowances had arrived and I had closed the mission books, I would fly with Gordon to Bangkok and await his return. So Merle made plans to go.

But it was not to be. When we returned from the International Church service on Sunday, there was another telegram at the door. Merle's father had died sooner than expected and the funeral was to take place the following day. The first telegram had arrived too late. A cousin volunteered to assist Merle's mother in his absence.

One night after 8 p.m., two young, neatly dressed Cambodian women came to our door. I knew neither of them.

"My husband is sick in the hospital," said one of them. "He has just received a telegram that his grandmother has died, and he needs someone to come and pray for her soul."

"My husband is not here," I replied. "He is teaching a class and may not be home for a while. Since curfew is at 9 p.m., it may be too late to come tonight."

"But someone must come and pray for his grandmother's soul."

It was a strange request, and I was perplexed. A Buddhist would not normally ask us to pray for a departed soul. They would call in the monks to chant.

"But you must come," the woman said with even greater urgency.

"I cannot promise. I don't know how soon my husband will return. Which hospital is your husband in?"

She gave me the name of a private clinic that I had never heard of, but the address was only a few blocks from the mission guesthome. "I'll be waiting for you," she said as she turned and walked away.

I suddenly realized that I had forgotten to ask her name. Who was she? Why was she so anxious for us to come? Was it a ruse? Maybe her husband was an American. What about the curfew? Would our search for the clinic after curfew cause suspicion and a reaction from the military? I was a bit apprehensive.

Nevertheless, I locked the door and waited on the front porch. Shortly before 9 o'clock, I saw our car turning into the driveway. I rushed down the steps, through the gate and out to the car. "Don't drive in until I tell you a story," I told Merle.

After listening, Merle replied, "We'll go."

"But curfew is only a few minutes away. Are you sure we should go?"

"We'll trust the Lord," he said.

Down the deserted street we drove, searching for a clinic that was supposed to be on the top floor of a building. Dim streetlights cast eerie shadows amidst the trees and foliage. We drove past the Army High Command without incident. About then we saw the form of someone standing on a second-floor balcony, waving. It was the woman who had come to my door. She had been waiting for us to arrive.

Since parking was not permitted on the boulevard, we drove to an unlit side street and nervously walked to the building. The first floor was deserted. We climbed to the second floor, and at the top of the stairs, the young lady met us and escorted us into a room where a young American man lay. (I will call him Randy.)

As Randy's story unraveled, we learned that his Christian grandmother had played an important role in his young life, but he had not heeded the things she had taught him. While serving as a pilot for a domestic airline in the Khmer Republic, Randy had met the beautiful young woman who had come to my door, and they were married.

While he was lying there in the clinic with typhoid fever, Randy had received a telegram stating that his grandmother had died. Memories of her flooded his mind, and he was grief-stricken. He had sent his wife to the mission to find someone to pray for his grandmother.

After hearing Randy's story, Merle said, "I would judge from what you have told me that your grandmother was a Christian. If so, she is now with Jesus. It's too late to pray for one departed. You are the one who stands in need of prayer." Randy gave thoughtful attention to Merle's words.

When Randy recuperated, both he and his wife began to attend the International Church. There, he surrendered his heart to the Lord. Esther Kroh, a nurse with the medical team and wife of Dr. Dean Kroh, invited Randy's wife to study with her, and she soon became a Christian.

We received a letter from Australia and New Zealand inviting us to minister for several weeks in some churches there. That meant we would be leaving Cambodia two months earlier than anticipated.

While speaking at a service in Auckland, New Zealand, I mentioned the valuable ministry of radio and particularly the encouraging response we had received to the Bible lessons in English that were beamed from the Far Eastern Broadcasting Company in Manila. I quoted excerpts from one of the letters of response that we received.

At the close of the service, to my surprise, a woman approached me. "I have a letter from the same person that you mentioned tonight. I am the one who writes the English lessons for that program. I can supply you with a list of those who have responded."

Excitedly, I took the names and sent them back to the Khmer Republic. In October we received a letter stating that one of the missionaries had visited the area from which many of the respondents had written. He found that fifteen out of the thirty correspondents were now firm believers, and he was able to establish a time and place for worship each Sunday afternoon.

At the conclusion of our ministry in Australia, we met Gordon in Bangkok. Within days, we were welcomed in New York by Ardelle, whom we had not seen for nearly four years!

20

A Great Cloud of Witnesses

April 17, 1975, marked the beginning of an infamous era in Cambodian history. We were in the US at the time, and Merle had gone north for some scheduled speaking engagements while Gordon and I remained in Toccoa Falls. I was home alone when the distressing news was aired around the world: The Khmer Republic had fallen to communist forces.

I fell on my knees before the Lord with tear-filled eyes. Many of our beloved brothers and sisters in Christ would face certain death. In submission to God's will, I could only say, "Though I may not understand, Lord, yet in Your sovereignty You do."

Our home assignment was quickly coming to a close. Fred and Marilyn and their family were on home assignment from Peru and were living on the same hillside as we were. There were two lovely grandchildren, Tim and Cheri, to get acquainted with. But we had planned, in due time, to return to the Khmer Republic.

Then came the disturbing news that all of the Cambodian missionaries had been evacuated. The Khmer Republic was cut off from the outside world. Glimpses of what occurred during the takeover were stunning beyond description. The new regime was more brutal than even the most pessimistic had predicted.

Though it was impossible to learn the fate of many of the Cambodian pastors and Christian leaders, refugees escaping the country brought bits of information concerning a few. Two of the elders from Bethany Church, Minh Thien Voan and Major Taing Chhirc, were apparently among the first Christian martyrs. Both had had opportunity to leave the country, but both had chosen to remain and minister in the name of Christ rather than choose the safety of an evacuation. Like Moses, they made their choice deliberately (see Hebrews 11:25-26).

Voan's wife and three children had been evacuated to Bangkok by World Vision. Dr. Mooneyham had urged Voan to depart also, but he had declined. He had parents and siblings who were yet unsaved. It was, perhaps, his last opportunity to witness to them concerning Jesus Christ.

A few years earlier, Voan's mother had had a vision in which she saw Christ hanging on the cross. Jesus said to her, "It is for you. I died for you." She had been moved, but had hesitated to take the necessary step of faith. Voan's father, who was employed by the Ministry of Education, had listened to Voan's witness but replied, "You have more wisdom than I." The day before the city fell, Voan spoke by radio to a staff member of World Vision. "My mother, three sisters and a brother-in-law have received Christ as Savior," he joyfully reported. "I am still praying for my father."

In a letter we received from Major Chhirc before he returned to Cambodia from Scotland, he had expressed the passion of his heart:

> Our dear Lord has given me unusual blessings and strength to overcome this world with its beauty, its pleasures and glory so that I could give up the security of life in Europe, my university degree and especially myself and make up my mind to surrender all and return. . . .
>
> My dear Lord Jesus is going to give me back to the Cambodian Church very shortly. He has led me in His wonderful way in the past months so that each minute has been very precious to me, enjoying the blessed fellowship of His Holy Spirit. How sweet it is to know and serve Him alone! Any human language is inadequate to describe it until the day when we'll be leaving our mortal and corrupted body, and there is no doubt that that day is very near. Since it is coming very soon, I couldn't stand the idea of having such a very small percentage of my fellow countrymen redeemed by the precious blood into our heavenly home. This is the purpose of my life on this earth.

After the country fell, Major Chhirc and Minh Thien Voan were reported to have taken refuge in the French Embassy. However, the Khmer Rouge ordered the embassy to evict every Cambodian in hiding there. Otherwise, they threatened that all food and water would be withheld from the embassy.

Major Chhirc and Voan then planned to head for South Vietnam. Several years later, a Christian reported that he had seen the two men at a Mekong River town in Cambodia in May 1975.[1] They had stopped to distribute copies of the Scriptures to the terrified and suffering populace. Khmer Rouge soldiers took them immediately, tied their hands and killed them with a blow to the head with a hoe.

Son Sonne, the dedicated and zealous soul winner, had continued to preach, teach and witness new churches spring up through his ministry. As director of the United Bible Societies in Cambodia, he was said to be contemplating evacuation with his family. However, he wanted to wait until the conclusion of the National Church Conference being held that April. It proved too late; the last commercial plane left. Driven from Phnom Penh into the countryside, Son Sonne became another casualty of the cruel regime.

In the closing days before the fall, Sin Sum, God's firebrand, had selected forty promising Christians for a short-term, intensive Bible study with morning, afternoon and evening classes. He had enlisted missionaries to assist in teaching. When news of the evacuation came, Sum said, "We can't drop the Short Term School. It is a month in duration. It must go on."

More than a year before, one of Sum's converts, a widow, had had a vision. She saw a ladder reaching from earth to heaven. It was glistening white with rungs of gold. Many people were going up the ladder, including Cambodians. Some were attempting to climb but were falling off. Sin Sum, already over halfway up, was leading the group, and heaven's gates were open to receive them. Christ was standing at the top of the ladder, flanked on either side by angels, as He smiled and awaited their coming.

Sin Sum desired to plant another church a few kilometers away. He had tried in one place without much response. He asked the widow, "Where was the foot of the ladder in your vision?"

"Over there," she replied, pointing in a certain direction.

"We'll try there," said Sin Sum. He did, and fifty-two persons prayed to receive Christ that Sunday. In a letter he wrote to us shortly before the country fell, he asked, "Will we see you again, and will it be here on earth or in heaven?"

No news was ever heard concerning Sum's fate. But one thing we know: Sin Sum had reached the top of the ladder.

Tuy Sreng, the pastor who had been a former Buddhist monk, was faithfully serving in an area that had been rather resistant to the gospel. As the Spirit of God began to move and converts started multiplying, an army general was reported to have said, "These Christians are going to overrun the city."

Sreng had witnessed the Lord's marvelous protection on many occasions. Though his wife survived the holocaust, he became one of the faithful martyrs.

An article entitled "Farewell to Cambodia" appeared in one of the US news magazines shortly after the fall of the country to the Khmer Rouge forces. An estimated 2 million Cambodians became victims of genocide, and thousands of others who fled were eventually scattered in various countries around the world. Yet God had not forgotten the Cambodian people. Thousands had found new hope and faith in Christ. Churches had continued to multiply in the Phnom Penh area, and the Holy Spirit was at work in provincial centers as well.

Only a few Christian leaders were able to escape. The majority became victims of genocide. Another generation of missionaries and national pastors are now witnessing the moving of God's Spirit once again in Cambodia, and today those heroes of faith who persevered until death are among that "great cloud of witnesses" (Hebrews 12:1) who surround us and cheer us on. The memory of their lives are a challenge to greater faith and obedience.

God truly had not forgotten the Cambodian people.

Note

1. Paul Penfold, "To Die Is Gain," *Cambodia for Christ*, no. 31, May/June 1980.

21

Sa Kaeo Camp

After the Cambodian people had endured nearly four years of the most brutal atrocities that one can imagine, the Vietnamese army moved in. Soldiers and civilians fled before the invaders, and an estimated 300,000 amassed on the Thai-Cambodian border. On October 24, 1979, this human dam broke and thousands poured into Thailand. Many were suffering and dying from malaria and a combination of other things, including pulmonary problems, severe malnutrition and tuberculosis.

At least 30,000 Cambodians were taken to a hurriedly prepared camp approximately 40 miles west of the border. They included Khmer communist soldiers and so-called sympathizers, so the camp was referred to as the Pol Pot Camp. Actually, many of the refugees were only the victims of circumstance. They had been caught up in the same web as the soldiers, or perhaps they had been slaves used to support the soldiers. But all of these people had existed for a time in the forests and jungles while making their way to the border. Many had not made it.

Relief agencies around the world responded to the refugees' needs. An International Christian Medical Team was formed, consisting of five evangelical agencies. They sent an emergency task force to the scene, headed by a Dutch Salvation Army major.

In November we received a telephone call asking if we would be available to go to Thailand to work in a refugee camp for a period of six weeks under the sponsorship of World Relief. Merle would be designated as chaplain of the medical team. At the time, we were living in Toccoa where Merle was senior pastor of First Alliance Church. The church board granted permission for him to leave, and we were soon on our way.

I was very excited about going to minister in the camp, but the timing was a disappointment, because it meant that we would not be home for Christmas. Since Marilyn and her family were home from Peru, we had been looking forward to having our entire family together for the first time in five years. It was finally agreed that we would celebrate in January after our return.

Sa Kaeo Camp was named after a small Thai town located about ten miles from the camp. It was in this town that the medical team was housed. Of necessity our days in the camp began very early—about seven people shared one bathroom! Breakfast was served at 7 a.m.

Walking into Sa Kaeo Camp was like walking into another world. Almost everything had been bulldozed, leaving only a layer of thick dust to cover our feet and swirl in the air, filling our nostrils. Germs

from diseases, spittle along the paths and open la-
trines made for a very unhealthy environment. Consequently, almost every staff member contracted
what was termed the "Sa Kaeo cough." The symptoms were a sore throat and a cough, which were difficult to overcome as long as one worked in the
camp. Merle and I both fell victim to it.

High barbed wire surrounded the camp, which
was guarded by soldiers night and day. Security was
exceedingly tight. Staff could enter only by submit-
ting proper identification, signing in each morning
at 8 a.m. and signing out each evening by 6 p.m.

Among the facilities at the camp were 8 hospital
wards accommodating 1,000 or more patients. Later,
a ninth ward was added. The hospital area was separated from the rest of the camp by another fence. We
could work freely in three of the wards and in three
others with discretion.

Armed with tracts, sometimes a wordless book, a
picture roll, a tape recorder and cassettes with messages in the Cambodian language, I made my way
each day through the sparsely furnished and ill-
equipped wards, their small wooden platform beds
lined up on either side of the rooms. The sad, gaunt
faces of the refugees lightened when they heard
someone speaking in their own language, someone
with whom they could share terrible memories,
heartaches and fears. Often they would indicate
their desire and readiness to accept Christ.

"I love the gospel and God," said a fifty-five-year-old
woman as she listened to a tape recording.

"Would you like to pray to receive Christ?" I asked.

"Yes," she replied.

A few beds away another woman called out, "I am ready to believe."

"This is heaven," said a patient as she lay upon her bed in the ward. Just the thought of having food and a safe place to lie down seemed sufficient for the moment.

Khieng, mother of four, had never heard the gospel message before coming to the camp, and she did not appear too responsive at first. However, a member of the medical team had been witnessing to the Red Cross volunteers who worked in the wards. One day the staff member approached Merle. "There are fourteen young Cambodian women waiting to receive Christ. Will you instruct them and pray with them?"

"Where is there a place large enough for that number to meet?" Merle asked.

"Perhaps we can arrange for use of the bathing area," the woman replied.

As Merle ministered to these young women, an additional four left their beds in an adjacent ward and began watching and listening through an open window. One of them was Khieng. When we visited her again, she was ready to put her faith in Christ. She willingly cut the devil string that she had worn for a long time in order to appease the devil.

Though unarmed, the Khmer Rouge in the camp still wielded some power by their presence and their threats.

Rin was a young woman about twenty-five years old. Separated from her parents, she had no relatives in the camp.

"Who are you living with?" I asked.

"The Khmer Rouge," she replied. "Can you help me to get out from under their control?" she whispered. "I don't want to be with them. Can I go back to the United States with you? I'll try so hard to learn English."

"I cannot help you, but I will pray for you," I responded.

After being dismissed as a patient, Rin was permitted to work in the World Vision ward at night, and living quarters in the camp were sought for her.

There was one orphanage section with 400 children, and over 30 were in another. Families had been separated by the Khmer Rouge, and these children had come to the camp without relatives. Since it was not known if any of the parents had survived, the children were listed as "unaccompanied minors." One of them, a downcast fifteen-year-old boy dressed in black, lamented, "I have no father, no mother. I'm all alone."

Another young lad was noticeably anxious to leave the camp. He had terrifying memories of his parents being stabbed in the throat with a knife. Then their stomachs were cut open and their livers removed. He had escaped by running to the mountains.

Not all of our experiences at Sa Kaeo Camp were bad, however. There was one particularly happy occasion when a father in the camp found his missing son there in the orphanage.

Thi (TEE) was a young girl, small and malnourished. She chattered meaninglessly into the air, revealing a disturbed mind and inner emotional conflict. Doctors pronounced her psychotic, while others called her crazy. Some suggested that she was demon-possessed.

Thi had been a normal ten-year-old girl when she and her family fell victim to the tortures of Pol Pot soldiers. Her father, mother and two young brothers were tied to trees and, in her presence, were slashed and murdered. It was reported that she had been forced to eat some of their livers. Tormented by fears and painful memories, Thi had been mentally and emotionally scarred. However, she did respond somewhat to our love and concern. Who could possibly understand the extent of the turmoil that existed in some of these young minds?

A young mother supervising in the orphanage cried as she shared her story. She had accompanied a very ill sister to the camp to seek medical help. Bringing only her youngest child and pregnant with another, she had left the two older children with her husband at a border camp. Her sister soon died and, grief-stricken, the woman wanted to return immediately to her family. But she had discovered that once inside the barbed wire of Sa Kaeo Camp, it was exceedingly difficult to leave. Though she continued to seek permission, she had heard nothing.

A thirty-three-year-old woman lay dying. Extremely thin, malnourished and with shaven head, she resembled a skeleton. A large amount of pus had been extracted from her lungs, and medicine dripped into her right arm while fluid rattled in her chest. Without the presence of anyone to love her, she was afraid. I played a taped gospel message for her, and one morning Merle and I sat by her bed. Merle held her hand while he quietly witnessed to her about Jesus. As he spoke, she suddenly nodded her head for a moment as though she understood.

Walking back toward the ward after lunch, we saw two men entering with a stretcher. Our fears were confirmed: This skeleton of a woman had died. We hoped that the gospel had not come to her too late.

Shortly after we arrived at Sa Kaeo Camp, our hearts were deeply moved to see a multitude of black-garbed people sitting stoically in the hot sun and waiting silently for their food rations (black was the color the Pol Pot regime required them to wear). They had learned that survival meant showing no emotion for the happenings around them. We saw them as lost sheep without a shepherd.

Our hearts yearned to work among these masses, but we had been warned that it was considered a communist camp. How would we be received? Would it be dangerous for us to venture out? "Nothing tried, nothing gained," said Merle.

We had no meeting place and no contacts in the camp. We took some tracts and a wordless book that I had made and set out to seek a place off the beaten path where we could witness. When all the tracts were dispersed and we had told the good news to the crowd gathered around us, several expressed interest in praying immediately for salvation. Merle announced, "All who are interested, please meet us at this same spot tomorrow." We left, wondering what would happen.

We didn't have long to wait. The following morning they were there, awaiting our arrival. Since the communists had destroyed all books and literature, the people were desperate for something to read. They followed us, begging for tracts and booklets. Sorrowful expressions turned into smiles. Soon we had definite contacts, people who were willing to open their humble shelters for services.

Sa Kaeo Camp was dotted with little makeshift tents—sticks stuck in the ground with plastic or thatch for roofs. A mat, a blanket or a piece of plastic served as a wall. The dirt floor was occasionally covered with cardboard or burlap sacks. We had to stoop to enter, and sleeping mats were laid down for us to sit on, although we soon learned that small stones on the ground made sitting for long periods extremely uncomfortable.

Lann Rin and his family lived in the first little tent where we held services. The entire family soon became Christians. Rin often followed Merle from meeting to meeting listening to God's Word. (Since coming to the United States, Lann has served for a number of years as a Cambodian pastor on the West Coast.)

Other meeting places included a large tent and a house that had a raised platform on either side of the room to accommodate a larger crowd. The people filled the room, squatted around the doorway and peeked in between the bamboo and thatch. Sometimes the host would tell us, "These people have come to accept the Lord. I have asked the old Christians not to attend today." The "old" Christians were those who had prayed a day or two previously.

As I sat gazing at their hungry faces, I thought of the words in Psalm 42:1-2: "As the deer pants for streams of water,/ so my soul pants for you, O God./ My soul thirsts for God, for the living God."

There were no Bibles to offer. We learned of someone in Bangkok who might possibly have Gideon New Testaments on hand. With great excitement, we went to Bangkok and returned to the camp with a supply in the Khmer language.

Merle chose a few men who appeared to be promising leaders, loaned each a tape player with a cassette and instructed them to evangelize by gathering their friends and neighbors to listen to the messages on the tapes.

One particular day, we were asked to hold a service in another little tent at 3:30 p.m. "Let's have the meeting later," suggested Merle. "It will be cooler then."

With perspiration running down her face, the new convert replied, "We don't worry about the heat. We'll endure. We just want to study the Word."

It was getting late when that meeting had finished, but Lann Rin insisted that we had to go to his tent for another service. "Some have been waiting there since 9:30 this morning to hear the Word," he said.

We went, and thirty-four prayed to receive Christ.

A surgeon working with the medical team had passed out Gospels of John in one area of the camp. One day he noticed a little tent with a cross displayed at the top. He and Merle went to meet the occupants. "We notice that you have a cross on your tent. What is the significance?" they asked.

"I have believed in God, and I want others to know," the man replied.

"Who led you to the Lord?" Merle inquired.

"I read the good news by Mr. John," the man replied (he was referring to the Gospel of John).

A few days later, a photographer entered a hospital ward and excitedly asked, "Have you seen all of the crosses out in the camp? There must be about twenty of them." Believers were using this symbol as a testimony of their newly found faith.

The Pol Pot regime had tried to stamp out all evidence of Christianity in Cambodia, but in this camp, which even contained some of the Pol Pot soldiers, a church had been born, and the cross had been lifted up as a witness.

Our departure was at hand. We had prayed with more than 560 persons for salvation. Merle appointed eight men to serve as a committee to aid the next chaplain who would come after him. The day before we left camp, a doctor's wife who was one of the new converts invited us to her tent. She had prepared tea and a delicious Cambodian dessert for us. She had also made some jam to present to us as a farewell gift. It was nicely wrapped, and I was amazed that she had found these items and deeply humbled to know that she had taken from her sparse rations to prepare all of that for us.

Merle and I arrived in Los Angeles tired and exhausted from long hours of travel. We checked into a hotel and looked forward to a restful night. Before retiring, we phoned our son, who was then a student at Toccoa Falls College, to inform him of our arrival time at the Atlanta airport the following day.

"Aren't you going to the funeral?" he asked.

"Whose funeral?"

"Grandpa Gerwig died, and the funeral is tomorrow afternoon at 1 o'clock," he replied.

I hurriedly placed a call to my parents' home and learned that my father had suffered a sudden heart attack and had gone immediately into the presence of the Lord. Attempts to reach us in both Bangkok and Hong Kong had failed. We quickly dressed, checked out of the hotel and took the first available flight. We arrived in Marion, Ohio, at noon the following day, just one hour before the service was scheduled to begin.

About ten months later, Merle returned to Sa Kaeo Camp. I was unable to accompany him since I now had the care of my mother. The camp had been moved to a new location and conditions were much improved. The church had continued to grow as others took turns ministering to the refugees.

How different the situation was this time! The church committee itself invited Merle to speak to an audience now totaling over 1,000. Each Sunday, Food for the Hungry moved all the equipment from their building to provide a meeting place for the church. There were now three choirs. Children sang and recited Scripture, and the young people had acquired several guitars and prepared a special Christmas pageant with costumes.

One woman who worked in the camp testified to the faithfulness of one of the martyrs in Cambodia. It was 1978, and her husband and several children had been killed. She and her one remaining child were forced to move on with a group of other Cambodians. In that group there was one young man who appeared different from the others. A Christian, he witnessed to the woman and eventually led her to the Lord. But the communists would not tolerate his testimony, and they came to take him away. Before leaving, the young man said to the woman, "I will soon be with the Lord. Be true to Him until death."

"I am saved today because of his testimony and godly life," she told Merle.

By life or by death, God had been and was being glorified through His faithful witnesses.

22

The Icing on the Cake

A great exodus of refugees was spilling over international borders, and among them were many Cambodians. Tens of thousands were being resettled from refugee camps in Thailand to other countries, and many had already come to the United States. The mission field was at our door, and once again the call came. We were invited to join Intercultural Ministries to work among Cambodian refugees living in the eastern half of the United States.

So, in 1984 Merle resigned as senior pastor of First Alliance Church in Milwaukee, Wisconsin (later relocated to Germantown). We moved to Springfield, Virginia, a suburb of Washington, DC. "This is like the icing on the cake," Merle remarked. "We can spend our remaining years before retirement working among the Cambodian people."

Merle's basic task was to coordinate the Theological Education by Extension program (TEE) for Khmer people living east of the Mississippi River. Center leaders were to be trained, and they, in turn, would teach classes for prospective pastors and Christian workers. In addition, scattered throughout the metropolitan area were several thousand Cambodians, and we soon began to take steps to plant a church, although we had yet to determine the most strategic location.

We visited English-language schools in order to meet any Cambodians who might be enrolled and we then followed up on those names and addresses. We also met a young lady who was ministering weekly to some Cambodian youth, and she joined our efforts in planting a church.

But there were many obstacles to confront. False cults, one in particular, had been working persistently among the refugees. Each family that we visited, almost without exception, reported that cult members had already been to visit them. Many of the refugees had already been baptized into the cult.

"We didn't know," some told us. "When we came to America, we assumed that all churches were the same."

"They have been so good to us," said one man. "My wife doesn't want to offend them now."

We wept inside, knowing that many hungry hearts had been so deceived.

We also had difficulty finding a convenient time to hold church services with everyone's work schedules so diverse and unpredictable, and we were having trouble securing a suitable meeting place that would require the least amount of busing.

Since the greatest concentration of Khmer was in Arlington, Virginia, the Arlington Memorial Church (later renamed Arlington Community Church of The Christian and Missionary Alliance) offered space for services. Merle rented a school auditorium for a Sunday afternoon, advertised that pictures of Cambodia would be shown on that date and brought in a Cambodian Christian layman as a speaker for the afternoon. We also announced the date when regular church services would begin in the church building. While the adults worshiped in their own language, Sunday school classes in English were held for the children and teens.

Some of the Khmer had a difficult time adjusting to American culture. The language proved an overwhelming barrier to many of the elderly. For those who were illiterate in their own language, learning a new one seemed an impossible and insurmountable task.

Not only did the refugees have to learn a new language, they also had to learn a new lifestyle. The typical refugee had not been accustomed to a refrigerator, a stove, an indoor bathroom, a plush mattress or water that runs from taps. They had not shopped at supermarkets.

Some had also supposed that America would be Utopia. They had come with no money and little more than the clothes on their backs. But they soon discovered that they could not live such a happy, carefree life as they had hoped. Rent and living costs were high, and they could not stretch their monthly welfare checks and food stamps to afford the necessities of life. Many who were unskilled could obtain only low-paying jobs. Widows became homesick for their homeland and for loved ones now gone or left behind. A few longed to return to Cambodia in spite of its poverty and unrest.

There were those who still suffered from nightmares and were haunted by terrifying memories. It was difficult to find even one family who had not suffered the loss of family members in the killing fields. They were a hurting people who needed our love and our Lord.

"I'm so lonely here," confessed one woman. "I can't speak English, so I can't talk to anyone."

There was also an upheaval in Cambodian family life. The Asian family is an extended family, and it is very close, but in America that family was dismantled. Many children had no father, and some had no mother either.

The teenagers soon became Americanized, but they were also required by their parents or guardians to remain loyal to their own culture in many respects. In addition, language barriers forced parents to turn to their children as liaisons with the outside world. Teens were caught in a bicultural conflict, trying to identify with two different social groups. "Who am I?" they wondered. Some rebelled and, feeling the need for acceptance, often became involved with the wrong friends, joined gangs and committed crimes. This provided the Church with an opportunity to serve as an extension of the nuclear family, to give counsel and to provide hope.

There was an immediate need for a lay pastor for the new church. In God's providence, we met a couple living in Maryland, both of whom had been school teachers in Cambodia. Hiepson (He-up-SAHN) and Sean (SEE-un) Kaysarn had found the Lord as their Savior through the ministry of First Alliance Church in Silver Spring, Maryland.

"I was raised in a Buddhist family," testified Sean. "As a child, I often attended the Buddhist temple with my grandparents. . . . But, as I considered the teachings of Buddhism point-by-point, doubts arose in my heart. . . . Finally, I realized that Buddhism does not change the heart, and life spiritually remains obscure.

"After I was married, my husband and I had long talks together about various religions. We made a decision not to get involved in any of them. . . . Life appeared to offer no hope at all. Then a very dramatic event occurred in Cambodia. The communists took over our country. Terrorism, murder, hunger and the separation of families still bring sad memories to haunt the Cambodian mind. We also had three innocent daughters indirectly killed during the regime.

"Coming here to a new country, we brought with us sorrow, loneliness and a feeling of uncertainty beyond expression. Spiritually, we had no destination. All of this made us think about our lives again. We worried much about our future, especially concerning our three remaining children.

"There were many churches in the area, but I did not know which one we should attend. So I started praying to God, even though I did not yet know who He was. I just prayed in my heart, 'You who created the world, the universe and mankind, show me the way, and tell me what to do.' "

Shortly thereafter, Hiepson and Sean met a lady who invited them to come to her church. In due time, the whole family had accepted the Lord as their Savior.

"We continually thank God," said Sean, "that He revealed to us the way of salvation . . . and that He had obedient servants whom He used to lead us to Him." Hiepson and Sean now wanted to serve the Lord in any way that He led. This was a definite answer to our prayers. Hiepson and Sean moved their family to Virginia and both enrolled in the theological education class that Merle taught.

I taught an English class to reach out to the women. Later, realizing the need for special music for worship services and programs, I asked Sean to teach the English class, and I began a music theory class for the youth. I also gave piano lessons and organized a youth choir and a musical ensemble. I spent many additional hours acting as an interpreter for refugees in government and social service offices and health clinics. We also planned God-honoring Christmas and Easter programs with fellowship dinners to reach out to the unsaved, plus church picnics in local parks and fundraisers to help teens raise money to attend youth conferences.

The city of Philadelphia became another priority project in reaching the estimated 8,000 Cambodians who had settled there. Again, God answered in a most unexpected and unusual way. The Christian owners of a factory expressed willingness to hire a Cambodian chaplain and give him the opportunity to have a spiritual ministry among their Khmer em-

ployees. A Cambodian Christian accepted this responsibility, and a church was established that later
mothered another congregation in the city.

In June 1987, we had just returned from the
Boston area where Merle had spoken at the Cambodian National Conference. The following morning,
he was taken by ambulance to the hospital. After
four failed attempts at angioplasty, emergency surgery was performed in order to save his life. While a
triple bypass was planned, only two bypasses were
completed because of excessive bleeding and a dramatic drop in blood pressure. After six days in intensive care and five additional days in the hospital,
Merle recovered.

It was now 1990, and we had served beyond the
normal age of retirement. I was still not ready to re-
tire, but the time had come to pass the torch on to
the next generation. Approximately twenty center
leaders had been trained and eighty students were
enrolled in the theological education program.

At the time of this writing, the Kaysarns still continue to lead the northern Virginia Cambodian congregation. Pastor Kaysarn was ordained at the Cambodian conference in 1999. Some of that original
youth group, including two of the Kaysarn children,
are now engaged in Christian ministry. The oldest
son, John, and his wife, Kannara, live in California.
John is presently serving as director of youth/young
adult ministries for the Cambodian district churches

(C&MA) in the US. The Kaysarns' daughter, Srey-leak, and her husband, Harald Hem, live in Norway. Harald is the affiliate coordinator for Mission Without Borders International.

We recall the testimony of a young man who had just graduated from the Ta Khmau Bible School: "I marvel in my heart at the greatness of His grace. It's beyond measure or expression. How can I ever repay Him? If I had a thousand lives to give Him, it wouldn't be sufficient."

Those words express the sentiments of our hearts as well. The work of God's kingdom will continue to prosper and bear fruit by those of succeeding generations who will believe that "nothing is impossible with God" (Luke 1:37).

Epilogue

Merle and Louisa Graven reside at the Alliance Community for Retirement Living in DeLand, Florida.

Marilyn and her husband, Dr. Fred Smith, spent three terms of missionary service in South America, first in Peru and then in Ecuador. Fred later served eight years as regional director for Latin America North for The Christian and Missionary Alliance and four years as regional director for Latin America (north and south combined), while Marilyn worked at the C&MA national office in the *Alliance Life* magazine circulation department. They are currently living in Toccoa, Georgia, where Fred is director of the School of World Missions at Toccoa Falls College. They have two children, Tim (married to Danel) and Cheri (married to Scott), and four grandchildren— Amanda, Caitlyn, Autumn and Josiah.

Ardelle was employed for a number of years in human resources management. She and her husband, Donald Liberman, are presently living in San José del Cabo, Baja, Mexico, where he is engaged in business.

Gordon married Janice Tinklepaugh, a teacher. They reside in Warwick, New York, and have one son, Christian. Gordon is director of operations for the Americas, Agfa Corporation's healthcare division.